UNAI
EMERY
EL MAESTRO

UNAI
EMERY
EL MAESTRO

THE AUTHORISED BIOGRAPHY
Romain Molina

Updated and translated edition published in Great Britain in 2018
by Tales From Publishing

© 2018 Tales From Ltd

This edition published by arrangement with Hugo & Co in conjunction
with their duly appointed agents L'Autre agence, Paris, France.

© 2017 Hugo Publishing

Translation by Nicholas Caistor

Printed and bound by CPI Group (UK) Ltd, Croydon, CR0 4YY

Jacket photograph (front)
©Alex Martin/Presse Sports

Jacket photograph (back)
© Robbie Stephenson/JMP/Shutterstock

Jacket design and typography by www.stonecreativedesign.com

ISBN 978-1-912249-05-3

Tales From Ltd
107 Jupiter Drive, Hemel Hempstead, Herts HP2 5NU
Registered company number: 9082738
www.talesfrom.com
info@talesfrom.com

UNAI EMERY: EL MAESTRO

CONTENTS

Introduction: 'The past isn't a weight'   7

1. Birds are Made to Fly, Man is Made to Work   13

2. All Skin and Bone   19

3.1 Free Kicks and Doubts   25

3.2 Interview with Luis Cesar Sampedro   33

4. Temple of the Sun   37

5. A Prophet in his Own Land   43

6. Earthquake in the Second Division   51

7. The Good, the Bad and the Ugly   57

8.1 A Throw of the Dice   65

8.2 Interview with Alvaro Negredo   73

9. The Legend of El Dorado   77

10.1	Afraid of No One	83
10.2	Interview with Juan Mata	93
11.	The Land of Shadows	97
12.	The Spy Who Played for Spartak	103
13.	Rekindling the Flame	111
14.	Conquering Europe	117
15.1	The Wonders of Seville	127
15.2	Interview with Adil Rami	137
16.	Living on a Volcano	141
17.1	To Descend into Hell, then Climb Out	153
17.2	Interview with Romain Grunstein	163
18.1	Live by the Sword…	167
18.2	Interview with Unai Emery	175
Career Statistics: Unai Emery		189
Acknowledgements		191

INTRODUCTION

THE PAST ISN'T A WEIGHT

'This is a club… with a pure atmosphere. Very pure.' Unai Emery is sitting calmly at his desk at Arsenal's training ground, in Colney, Hertfordshire. Two days earlier, he had won his first game as the Gunners' manager, beating West Ham 3-1. 'You always sleep better with a win,' he jokes. 'Yesterday, I went to see Watford versus Crystal Palace. I'd already been to Wembley for Chelsea-Manchester City (the Community Shield). Whenever I have a free day, I take advantage to travel and go to stadiums. You always see something new from inside the ground… Besides, I like football, that's all there is to it. So in London, I'm spoilt for choice!'

Since his start as a manager, with Lorca in the Spanish *Segunda B* (third division), Unai has had a spectacular rise, with only one failure – the months spent at Spartak Moscow. 'Yes, yes, but I learnt from it,' he insists. 'Any experience should help you to learn, from what you do well but also from your mistakes.' As proof, after quitting Moscow he went straight to Seville, where he won three Europa League titles, then PSG, one of the most ambitious clubs in Europe, and now Arsenal, a historic club that is famous worldwide. 'I couldn't see myself taking a season out,' the Basque manager goes on, the words pouring out of him. 'Coming to Arsenal… is a mixture of things. On the one hand it's a great, a very great club, with an important past and culture. On the other, it's a challenge, that I'll face with the staff, the players, the employees, the bosses and the fans. I'd like to say more, but we're only just at the start of this adventure. Apart from the hard work and the excitement at the novelty, I don't yet have much to say *(smiles)*.'

On 23 May 2018, Unai was officially appointed as the successor to Arsène Wenger. The Frenchman left the club after a 22-year reign, leaving an incalculable legacy similar to that of Sir Alex Ferguson at Manchester United. 'But it's a different situation,' says Luis Fernández, former European champion with France in 1984 and winner as manager of the European Cup-Winners' Cup in 1996 with PSG. 'There is pressure when a manager follows on from such big names, but even when you're not replacing a famous manager, there's still pressure, it goes with the job! *(laughter)*. David Moyes is a good manager but he didn't have the experience of European Cup finals or of a team like United where there's an obligation to win, international stars and a pretty charged atmosphere. Unai though is equipped for all that. Besides, Arsenal have a lot of young players, who fit in well with his philosophy, his way of working. He's very meticulous, as I saw at PSG last season (Fernández is the sporting director at their youth academy), he works very hard. He helped people like Rabiot, Kimpembe and Areola develop, and brought in young players like Weah or N'Soki. I may be wrong, but the choice of Arsenal looks good for both sides.'

Obviously, comparisons between Arsène Wenger and Unai Emery are flying about, as if it was essential to decide 'who's best'. It's obviously a crucial question for certain footballing debates that don't hesitate to compare players from the 1960s or 1970s (Pelé, Maradona...) with the new stars of the 21st century, with the implication that football has stayed the same. It's a theory like any other, but poor Charles Darwin would be tempted to come back from the dead to see just how far the *beautiful game* has evolved. It changes with each passing day: what worked yesterday may not work tomorrow, leading to new tactics, ways of playing and of coaching players.

In that regard, Arsenal announced that Unai was being appointed 'head coach' rather than 'manager' as Wenger had been, signalling the club's slow metamorphosis. Already in November 2017 the club structure had been upset: Sven Mislintat (ex-Borussia Dortmund) was named chief scout, and Raul Sanllehi (ex-Barcelona) appointed head of football relations. From now on, recruitment will not simply be left to the *head coach*, although obviously he will be consulted; but above all he will be expected to train the players, not to deal with agents, contracts, negotiations and other little things of the sort.

Mislintat and Sanllehi were part of the think-tank tasked with finding Wenger's successor. Both of them worked with Ivan Gazidis, the chief executive, and interviewed potential coaches (Mikel Arteta, Massimiliano Allegri…), among them Unai Emery, who came to the meeting with Javi Garcia, his goalkeeper trainer at Seville and PSG, called in for the day to be Emery's English-Spanish interpreter. 'We talked for several hours,' Emery confirms. 'It was intense, fascinating. They explained their project and their needs, and I gave them my vision of football and of Arsenal.'

Mad about football, to the extent that Edinson Cavani speaks of him as 'one of the most passionate people I've seen in this sport,' Unai gave his analysis of each Arsenal player, as if he already knew the squad's strong and weak points.

That comes as no surprise to Juan Sanchez, who was sporting director when Emery was at Valencia: 'When I interviewed him for the job, he knew the team better than the people working at the club' *(laughs)*. Except this time, Emery had competition. In all his other jobs, the clubs might have had other possible candidates, but he was always more or less the favourite. That wasn't the case at Arsenal, who logically enough had already circled the names of several well-known managers.

'It was a new situation for Unai,' says Igor Emery, his younger brother who takes cares of several things for him (relations with the press, analysis prior to games and other matters), 'He had to convince, almost to sell himself, *(laughs)*. More seriously, he took Javi with him for the initial meeting. Then, once Arsenal had made their decision and appointed Unai, they asked us to go to Atlanta to meet the owner, Stan Kroenke. We flew there and were driven straight to meet Mr Kroenke. His son was with us, and we talked for just a little while because he had a very full agenda, but it was important to meet him in person. Then we went straight to the airport and flew back to London. A few hours later, Unai was presented to the press. We were all exhausted, we didn't really have time to prepare anything *(laughs)*. Unai had a shower, changed clothes and off we went.'

Igor is a discreet man, who turns down most requests from the media – something that caused him headaches with certain journalists in Paris, who accused him of being the family's éminence grise or 'guru'. 'We did hear that nonsense,' protests one of the senior management team at PSG, 'but they must be sick to think that.' Wishing to remain anonymous, he goes on: 'I've only met Igor Emery once in my life. The Emery's don't make any noise, they stay away from cameras, and they don't do any politicking: in this club, that's exceptional. One could criticise Unai and his staff for lots of things – I myself have several bones to pick with him – but there are two things about which there's nothing to be said: their integrity and their honesty.'

In recent months, Igor has successfully obtained his coaching diplomas, writing a thesis on the importance of throw-ins. 'It's a frequent occurrence in a game, and it offers many possibilities, sometimes to get out of being pressured, or even to offer a goalscoring opportunity. Of course, I looked at Rory Delap's long throw-ins for Stoke City, but also the way Bielsa, Guardiola, Sarri or my brother prepared for them. Don't forget, it was from a throw-in that Seville qualified for one of the Europa League finals, with a goal by M'Bia in the last minute at Valencia…'

Igor will himself become a manager one day, but sometime in the future. For now, he's assisting Unai and helping him to the best of his ability. 'I went with him for the pre-season tour in Singapore. I saw how much hard work he put in. As we left the plane, he told the squad: 'We'll pass by the hotel, then straight to training.' The humidity made the heat impossible, it was the middle of the day, after such a long voyage, and yet none of the players protested. That was a positive sign, even if everything looks rosy when a new coach arrives. What I mean is that the players are open to changes, to question themselves and to make an effort. The training was intense, I was very glad I didn't have to do it *(laughs)*.' This feeling was shared by several players, taken aback by the amount of work they had to do, particularly the videos.

'When I launch a project, we trace a path to follow, both individually and collectively,' Unai explains. 'For now, I'm pleased with the work atmosphere, but as I said, the adventure is only just starting. What I've most enjoyed personally is to discover the club's history. I've been shown the trophies, the legends... it's easy to see everything that Arsenal means. I don't know if this is typical of English football, which society views differently than in France, for example. Here, I quickly became aware of the impact that football has on people's lives. Not everyone, of course, because some don't like football, but in general there's a very strong link between a team and their fans' lives. That means I feel a responsibility, and so do the players, but it's also stimulating, exciting. Honestly, who doesn't like to play in a packed stadium and to feel the love that people have for football? By that I mean the players, the club employees, the bosses, the fans, everyone.'

The first weeks of training and competition were marked by individual chats with every player, as is usual for most new trainers. On several occasions, Unai asked his players to tell him why they played football, what they hoped for from Arsenal, and from life in general. 'First of all, I have to understand the man, otherwise I'll never completely understand the player,' says Emery.

So, he constantly encourages someone like Alexandre Lacazette, whom he was already interested in at PSG. This isn't a guarantee of success, but it's the way Emery works. 'There's bound to be a barrier between the coach and the players, because we think there are certain limits that shouldn't be crossed,' explains Juan Carlos Carcedo, his faithful assistant manager. 'But every day the two of us discuss the best way to manage each individual. I mean as a person; the player always comes afterwards. Football is above all about human beings. If you start treating them like machines, or being with no feelings or emotions...' He pauses for a moment, then mentions the case of Edinson Cavani, one of the most atypical characters in the modern game, someone who is incredibly generous off the pitch and who, on it, will run like five people, while still having the selfish streak of a striker.

'We've met all sorts in our career,' says Juan Carlos, 'the temperamental, the sensitive, the angry ones, the egoists, players who couldn't give a damn, party animals, players who are half-asleep, or hyper-active, some really good guys... And the fact that we've trained players in different countries and of all nationalities also gives us greater understanding of players.'

All of which should stand the pair in good stead with the Gunners' cosmopolitan squad, with 15 different nationalities and their wide variety of characters. 'There's a desire, enthusiasm and a willingness to learn. That's the most a coach can ask for,' concludes Unai, before returning, as ever, to his task.

'He came to dinner last winter,' Luis Fernández recalls. 'We had our meal and there was a game on the TV – I can't remember exactly which one. Unai lived it as if he were on the pitch. We spent the whole evening talking football, players, his plans... I've been lucky enough to know some of the masters of the sport, people like Marcelo Bielsa, men of their word, men with principles. I put Unai in the same category, honest people, the sort who are becoming increasingly rare in football. For a year, I saw him arrive every morning and leave every evening, respecting every PSG employee and the club as an institution. That's why I can understand Arsenal's choice. Arsène's legacy has to be respected, his successor has to show humility following on from such a towering figure, while at the same time adding his own contribution.'

This is obviously easier said than done, but Unai has already been through a lot: injuries, doubts, anguish, the quagmire of the Spanish *Segunda B*, boos and whistles at the Mestalla, solitude in Moscow, the fervour of Seville and the follies of Paris.

'It's a great story, a story that deserves to be told,' says Alberto Benito, one of his friends who was his sporting director at Almería. 'People don't know Unai Emery. He smiles at press conferences, he's always positive, and he gets carried away on the touchline: that's there for the whole world to see. But behind all that, there's something more, the evolution of a man.'

1

BIRDS ARE MADE TO FLY, MAN IS MADE TO WORK

'When the sun shines after rain, it's magnificent. It brings out the green all around us, the sea, the mountains [...] I often used to miss the first hour of school in the morning. I preferred to go to the market at seven to see the catch the fishermen had brought in. I could spend an hour watching them, to see whether they were anchovies or tuna...' Unai Emery loves to talk about his region. For the cookery programme *No es país para sosos* (*It's not a land for slackers*), he returned to his birthplace, Hondarribia, a town of some 16,000 inhabitants bordering the Bay of Chingoudy, which forms a natural frontier between Spain and France. It is a place still preserved from developers in a beautiful natural setting, greatly appreciated by city dwellers at holiday periods.

'Every summer we have lots of tourists, especially people from Madrid,' explains Igor Emery, the youngest of the four brothers, eight years Unai's junior. 'The town hasn't really changed since we were boys. It's grown a little bigger, but not much. The heart has stayed the same.' Known in French as Fontarrabie, its charm comes from the Marina, the historic fishermen's quarter with its brightly painted cottages, and the central ramparts. Looking at them, they seem ageless, and it's true. Neither time nor man can really change the town, and that's why Hondarribia is so beautiful. It may not be very big, but visitors often get lost in it. The reason lies in the narrow, steep streets, whose bends, or so they say, allow people to sober up after the *txikiteo*, a tradition in northern Spain that consists of drinking small glasses of wine in each of the town's bars.

'My childhood here was very happy,' Unai goes on to say, sitting with a bottle of wine in front of him. It's drunk with slices of bread and fresh red mullet at a table with the co-presenters of the TV programme, the chefs Ramón Roteta – who also comes from Hondarribia – and Ander González. In the middle of this food programme, Unai can't help slipping in an allusion to football 'this sport played almost everywhere'. It has to be said that the Emery family is linked heart and soul to the round ball and to their region, Gipuzkoa, one of the seven historical provinces of the Basque country.

In this little enclave tracing the border with France, Real Sociedad and the Real Unión Club of Irun were two members of the first official Spanish national *Liga* in 1929. They competed with their neighbours (the Athletic Club in Bilbao and the Arenas Club in Guecho) in a championship of ten clubs eventually won by Barcelona ahead of Real Madrid. Sound familiar? It's not quite what it seems: the two super-powers hadn't yet colonised Spanish football, especially not Madrid: it was the Basque country that occupied the throne. The silver medal won at the 1920 Antwerp Olympic Games was won by a group of 19 players of whom 13 were Basques, most notably the legendary striker Pichichi, whose name has passed down to posterity because a trophy named after him is awarded each year to the top goalscorer in the Spanish championship. At the time, Bilbao was also the club that won the most Spanish Cups (7) and Irun wasn't far behind, winning it in 1913 and in 1918.

Stuck nowadays in the third division, this frontier club six kilometres from Hondarribia is one of the historic giants of Spanish football, providing a host of international players, among them Patricio Arabolaza. 'He was born and died in Irun,' explains Carlos Fernández, historian and former president of Real Union. 'He scored Spain's first goal at the Antwerp Olympics and was the symbol of the *furia*. What is the *furia*? Following the third-place match that Spain won 3-1 against the Netherlands, a Dutch journalist used the term '*furia*' to describe the Spanish way of playing. While it's true that Arabolaza and his teammates had the annoying habit of giving bear hugs even if their opponents didn't like it, it would be a mistake to reduce Spanish football and its Basque clubs to such rustic tactics. 'In the twenties and thirties, Irun had the best midfield in Spain, if not the whole of Europe, with Petit, Gamborena and Eguiazábal', according to Fernández. He picks out the French-Spanish player René Petit, an engineer by profession, as having had a great influence on the game in his time. In 1924, he was the one who led his team to the final of the Spanish Cup against his former club, Real Madrid. Yet the history books mention above all the presence of Steve Bloomer,[1] the English coach and the first big star of world football, who was one of several British pioneers who helped Spanish football considerably. Bloomer relied on the local talent, not really having any choice in the matter: professional football only became legal in 1925, and only the stars of the time could live without also having a job.

At the heart of Bloomer's team was a 19-year-old railway worker and budding goalkeeper called Antonio Emery. 'Our grandfather,' says Igor with a smile. 'It's with him that our family's love story with football begins…' Love strikes out of the blue, and there's nothing to be done in the face of destiny. For Antonio, this love affair was difficult at first; he was probably not expecting it. In the morning, he was meant to be playing on the left-wing, but then Irun's first-choice goalkeeper Muguruza pulled out due to a sudden illness. That afternoon, Antonio saw the opposing team's striker bearing down on him. It was the kind of clash a man cannot forget, an impromptu encounter that happened again and again throughout his career. His short stature didn't matter (he was only 1.70 or 1.73 metres (5 foot 8 inches)) tall according to the archives): he was the 'Pajarito' (literally, the 'little bird'): a goalie who rushed out to face

---

1   Bloomer scored 331 goals for Derby County at the turn of the 20th century. A brilliant striker, he was imprisoned in Ruhleben internment camp near Berlin at the start of the First World War, together with Fred Pentland, who went on to become coach at Bilbao. The two men got permission to organise football games in the camp, forming a federation, a championship and cups. Bloomer's story is told in full in Peter Seddon's book, *Destroying Angel: Steve Bloomer: England's First Football Hero.*

every danger and who, so the legend goes in the Basque country, flew above his opponents to punch the ball clear.

During the final of the Spanish Cup in 1924, the Madrid forwards swore that the heavens were on his side. Who knows? In the former Real Sociedad stadium, the Estadio de Atocha, his teammate José Echeveste scored the only goal to make it Irun 1-Madrid 0. 'Playing against Madrid was like going to the scaffold', recalled Juan Emery, Antonio's son, for the sporting daily *As* in 2008. 'But my father spoke of Real Union's great quality. Their game was dazzling, a bit like Barcelona's today. Besides, most of the players were from Irun, and close friends [...] My father was good, but the one who stood out from the rest was René Petit. He never trained with the team because he was studying in Madrid. Every weekend he would get on his motorbike and race to Irun. His talent made up for the lack of training. He was sensational.'

Three years later, they reached the final again, this time against Arenas de Guecho in Zaragoza. Different opponents, different venue but the same heroes: Petit captain, Emery the invincible goalkeeper and Echeveste the only scorer, in extra time. This meant a second cup win for Antonio, one more than his brother Ramón, the winner in 1918 and unfortunate finalist in 1922 against Barcelona (1-5), when he was captain.

In the Basque country, many people wanted to see Emery chosen for the national side despite the prowess of the divine Ricardo Zamora, the first (rock) star of Spanish football. But the rules meant Emery wasn't eligible – because his father was French. He stayed with his beloved local club, playing in the very first *Liga* of 1929. And thanks to an irony of fate, he was the first goalkeeper to have a goal scored against him in the history of the Spanish championship. This was at the Sarriá stadium, the former home of Espanyol, on 10 February 1929. The executioner went by the name of José Prat, alias '*Pitus*', another mythical figure, who had the brilliant idea of scoring only once in the whole season. A gentle irony, like that of Antonio's nickname '*Pajarito*'. According to his son Juan, this wasn't just because of his agility in the air. It was because in order to start playing against Santander, he had to give up his true passion: feeding little birds...

Juan Emery, in fact, was also a goalkeeper, who played all over Spain, from La Coruña to Huelva, passing through Irun. 'He talked to us a lot about football. Above all, he liked playing with us, giving us little training sessions. Even when we were small, we already had a football at home,' says Igor, keen like his three brothers to imitate dad and grandad. 'Obviously, the Emery family were known as a family of footballers in the village,' according to their childhood friend and football coach Mikel Jauregi. 'I first knew Unai when he was about ten years old because I was his coach in the Hondarribia youth team. We also met outside football because my parents were friendly with his. I remember his father often told stories about football and that fascinated him.' Going into commerce after a career with nine clubs, Juan left the impression of being a good, upright man. Many people in the football world were moved by his death in May 2015 at the age of 82. 'We received numerous telegrams and messages from many clubs, which was touching. Our father was acknowledged as a sportsman but also as a human being, which is even better,' says Igor.

Alongside Juan in the family photographs is Amelia, the only woman in the household. 'You might ask how she could manage with four boys, but that shows you don't know her, she's a strong woman. She doesn't stand any nonsense, that's for sure. And she's one of the characters of Hondarribia. She's in the habit of going every day to the beach for a while, even in January or February. And I mean every day! She says it's good for the health.' Her advice has other benefits. Facing the azure infinity of the Atlantic, winter allows you to listen to the surrounding silence, interrupted only by the seductive sounds of the waves on the shore. You only have to close your eyes and let your mind wander back through time. Here, almost a century ago, a young railway worker must have flown on the sandy beach. And you can be sure it's not a legend: '*el Pajarito*' was really flying.

2

ALL SKIN AND BONE

Unai Emery didn't continue the family line of goalkeepers. Nor did his brothers, apart from Igor. 'I did everything a bit differently from my elders,' Igor laughs. 'They all studied at a Basque school, but you could say they weren't the best students in the world. Seeing I was much younger than them, my parents wanted to do things differently. They enrolled me in a school at Hendaye in France because they had high hopes for me and thought being able to speak French would be useful. After that, I was at Saint-Jean-de-Luz and then at Pamplona University in Spain. I always played football, until I had a cruciate ligament injury. That affected me, above all, mentally because I really wanted to be a professional. So I chose to study journalism in order to be able to stay close to that world [...] After rehabilitation I returned to football but didn't play that often. I was in the *Tercera* (the Spanish fourth division), then played for Fontarrabie until the ligaments in my other knee gave out. I had some more small injuries, and retired when I was twenty-five. My other brothers had stopped playing when they were eighteen or twenty, except for Unai.'

All the brothers, including Unai, were hooked on football from an early age. The only difference perhaps was that he fell for it hook, line and sinker, without anyone noticing, one Sunday evening. 'There was always a football match on the TV, and I would watch it through the half-open door of the living-room. I'd watch as much as I could until Mum came out and told me: "Go to bed, it's late and you've got school tomorrow", he wrote in his 2012 book on management and psychology, *Mentalidad Ganadora, el Metodo Emery* [*A Winning Mentality, the Emery Method*]. Curiously, it's not his father who introduced Emery to football, but the opposite. 'He never threw a ball for me to play with. Of course, there was a favourable family attitude, but I was immediately interested on my own account. I liked to go to the grounds to watch matches. I must have been four or five at the time… I remember we used to go with my father and brothers to a pitch near our house where we played until nightfall. It's true I was more interested by football than by school at that age…' Thanks to this practice with the ball, Unai became a good left-footed player. 'But he wasn't so good with his right, I seem to remember,' jokes Mikel Jauregui. 'He was skinny, introverted, but he had an excellent technique. He was a very respectful kid, but above all very thin. That's the first thing that comes to mind when I think back to that period.'

This opinion is shared by Mikel Extarri, who knew him from the youth teams at Real Sociedad, the biggest club in the region, which Unai joined as an adolescent. 'He was all skin and bone. I was almost afraid he would be snapped in two. He played in the left midfield… I've got loads of memories of him, but one in particular stands out, during a tournament in Easter Week. We usually picked a team from the region, and Unai, who at that point was playing for the second youth team, was chosen. We were playing an Italian club, Fiorentina if I remember rightly. I left him on the bench in the first half, and he seemed unsure, doubtful of his own ability. I told him he would play in the second half, and that he was going to score. And incredibly, that's what he did! Unai was a good player, but he definitely wasn't a goalscorer…' It may only have been a tournament, but it already encapsulates his future career as a footballer: obvious talent but a hesitant personality. Unai confirms this, describing himself as '*cagón*' (shit-scared). 'One day a coach shouted at us in the dressing room: "Haven't you lot got any balls?" And I replied: "Yes, but they're worn out!"'

Despite his fears, Unai progressed through the ranks of the youth teams without making much noise, except to his trainer. 'A lot of trainers don't like it when a player, and especially a young one, questions their decisions. But I used to love it! That shows the kid is interested and wants to get on. I used to explain to him why we were doing a particular exercise or routine. He had a constant desire to learn.' says Extarri, delighted to share his memories. Now over 70, the 'wise old sage' as some here call him, is a selector for the Basque country. Before that, he was with Real Sociedad for more than 18 years, from technical director to reserve team coach, often giving talks on tactics and psychology to train the trainers. In 2003, he published an important book: *Manual de Futbol: desarrollo de conceptos tácticos en distintos sistemas de juego.* 'The work of Mikel Extarri and Jesús Zamora[2] has been appreciated, admired and, what matters most, put into practice by many trainers for years,' writes Raynald Denoueix in the book's introduction. Of all the coaches Unai had during his footballing career, it was perhaps Extarri who had the greatest influence on him. 'It would be pretentious of me to claim that, but I'm sure he liked my style and the way I approached football. Seeing him progress is… *[a lengthy pause]* he's always stayed in touch, asking my advice, a bit like Julen Lopetegui (currently the manager of Real Madrid). When he didn't have a club after his experience in Moscow, he came to the school where I give lessons on tactics. He sat with the other students without saying a word and took notes. On another occasion I asked him to give a talk, and he was happy to do so. I saw him as an adolescent and I see him now when he's over forty, and he hasn't changed a bit. He's still passionate about football, and still just as thin!'

Unai lived that passion to the full when 'his' Real Sociedad were Spanish champions in 1981 and 1982 and lost in the semi-finals of the European Cup to Hamburg (2-3 on aggregate) the following year. 'One of his role models was Roberto López Ufarte, a very quick left-winger who could do amazing things with the ball. He was a bit like Unai, not very strong or tough in duels on the pitch,' according to Extarri. The son of Spanish parents and born in Fez,

---

2 Jesús María Zamora spent his entire career as a midfielder at Real Sociedad, playing over 450 games in *La Liga* before moving up to become a youth team trainer.

Morocco, Ufarte moved to the Basque country when he was eight. Ironically, he began his footballing career at Irun, before moving to Real Sociedad. That was the start of a golden decade for the club under Alberto Ormaetxea and then the Welshman John Toshack, who left the club for two seasons to manage Real Madrid where he won two championship titles before returning in 1991. Early in the 1990s, the *txuriurdin* were always involved in European competitions and welcomed their first international player of the modern age: John Aldridge, the former Liverpool striker. Other English players followed, notably the Arsenal midfielder Kevin Richardson, as well as Portuguese players and some from Eastern Europe, such as Valeri Karpin, and the Mexican star 'Doctor' Luis García Postigo, who had the worst season of his glorious career (two goals in ten games) at the Atocha. In this context, it wasn't easy for young players like Emery, stuck in the reserve team that played in *Segunda B*. 'Unai arrived here at the wrong moment. Above all, he had an injury that unsettled him, and he was replaced by Javi de Pedro. He was younger, and they both played in the same position. Javi went on to play for the national team (winning 12 caps), so Real didn't make a mistake. Unai had talent, but maybe he was too much of an individualist. Javi passed the ball better,' says Extarri.

While Pedro went into the first team, Emery played 95 games over five years in the B team, a total affected by a recurrent knee injury. 'On the field, he was a bit like the coach. He was a veteran of the *Sanse*,' (the nickname for the reserve team) as Salva Iriarte explained to *El Desmarque*. Iriarte was Toshack's assistant, who became head coach when the Welshman was sacked. At the start of the 1995-96 season he brought Unai into the squad and gave him his chance during the eighth game, against Mérida (losing 1-2). Sacked in his turn, Iriarte was replaced by Javier Irureta, who used Emery as substitute in several matches. Five altogether, with one goal, during his last appearance in their blue and white shirt. 'It was against Albacete. The team was winning 5-1 when Unai came on. During one attack down the right-hand side, he ran as fast as he could and met the centre with his head. An unstoppable goal. That was a famous day: we won 8-1, and Unai scored with a header. We were on top of the world,' laughs Etxarri.

Emery was so happy he asked the Romanian Gica Craioveanu, who scored a hat-trick, if he could keep the match ball instead of him. His request was accepted, as an early leaving present: a few weeks later, Unai said goodbye to the *Liga* and his Basque country.

3.1

FREE KICKS AND DOUBTS

'To think we roomed together... how long ago? More than twenty years now. I'm going to feel even older just thinking of all that!' says Alberto Benito with a smile. From Cyprus, where he was sporting director of Anorthosis for a few months, he remembers his playing career in the youth teams at Real Madrid and then in the reserves at Valencia, Toledo and Cádiz. 'I arrived at Toledo in 1994, when the club was in the second division. Unai signed later on (in 1996). We got on from the start because we had shared tastes, especially a passion for football. Then we gradually roomed together.'

Club Deportivo Toledo was the second stop in Emery's career, and his first experience far from home, far from his beautiful Hondarribia. 'Leaving never prevented me from coming back, quite the opposite,' he likes to repeat, delighted to return for a few days to greet the Virgin of Guadalupe, the town's patron saint. 'He couldn't stay any longer at Real Sociedad. He was growing older and needed to play, to fulfil himself. He made the right choice,' says Etxarri. When he joined Toledo, Unai discovered a very different atmosphere. Basque football was known for its *furia,* but it was nothing compared to the work rate demanded by Juan Martínez, known as 'Casuco', born in Lorca in the south of Spain. 'I was reckoned to be a good runner; people said I had four lungs. Then I came to Toledo and I've never suffered so much physically. Never. I wonder if the coach wasn't an athletics teacher,' recalls Fabrice Henry, a runner-up in the French first division with Olympique Marseille in 1994.

'We had two training sessions a day when we hardly even touched the ball. We used to have to carry a player on our back and run to the halfway line. It was crazy, I've never seen anything like it. I would go home, and my then partner would make pasta, but I could only eat half before I wanted to go to bed.' In his book, Emery adds prosaically: 'We sweated blood.' Henry was one of the few foreigners in the group, together with the Serbs Aleksandar Radovic and Petar Divic. 'The president told me I was the first Frenchman in the club's history. I came here because I had just lost my brother and wanted to leave France. I wanted to forget everything, to start afresh somewhere else… I still had two years on my contract with Toulouse, but I went to see Alain Giresse, the manager, and told him I couldn't stay any longer. I signed for Toledo to recover, without thinking about the money – I earned 10,000 francs and had to pay rent of 5,600. It wasn't always easy, particularly because I spoke poor Spanish.'

Twenty years have passed, and memories of those days come and go as we talk. One name stands out: Unai Emery. 'I can't stand all those bastards who are full of it when someone becomes famous. I couldn't give a damn that he's famous now, although, of course, that makes me really happy. But what I'm telling you is the absolute truth. When I was with Toledo, the guy who helped me most was Unai. It was twenty years ago, but how could I forget him? I shared lodgings with him, and he always raised my spirits because I often thought of my dead brother and my family, which I lost when I was young. He was already a great human being. He gave me so much… he was a sort of shrink for me, always stressing the positive: "You'll see, Fabrice, everything will be all right!" I was a foreigner, and he could have had nothing to do with me. But no, that guy was always there.'

Benito confirms this description of Unai; 'He was a real fellow teammate, one of those who everyone in the dressing room liked because he was honest. You could tease him, joke around with him, he accepted it all with a laugh.' Emery came to the fore as a player as well, playing 37 games in his first season, which saw Toledo come 14th and brought a change of manager. That was a common occurrence with the *Verdes*. During his four years there, Emery played under Casuco, Emilio Cruz, Gregorio Manzano ('I liked his calmness, it was catching'), Miguel Angelo Portugal ('a master on keeping possession and of ways of training') and Luis Sanchez Duque. 'Like many clubs in the Spanish second division, it wasn't exactly stable,' confirms Benito, one of the first-team midfielders. 'Unai also played a lot. He was a rapid winger, good with the ball at his feet. But mentally, there was something lacking. He was weak on that level. As soon as there was any pressure, he couldn't take it.'

This weakness was a constant ever since his early days with Real Sociedad, and something he never managed to overcome as a player. 'It's true he doubted himself. In training he could make a great difference, but he wasn't very confident of his ability. And yet he was very strong technically, a really good player. I recently read an article that said he had no career as a footballer, that he was no good... but I'd like to have seen the cretin who wrote that on the pitch. I've played at Sochaux, at OM, Toulouse, Basel, at Hibernian, and all the French national sides apart from the first-team, so I think I've got the right to say he was a good player. He did have a footballing career, not like José Mourinho,'[3] insists Henry.

For the 1999-2000 season, Toledo showed its ambition by signing several top international names. The most surprising was the loan of Léider Preciado from Racing Santander. He was the only Colombian to score in the 1998 World Cup finals. Unfortunately, the great player from Cali didn't make any impact, scoring only one goal for the club. That was a nightmare year for Toledo, despite the winter arrival of Luis García, who went on to win the Champions League with Liverpool five years later. The inevitable relegation to *Segunda B* led to a mass exodus, including Emery. 'His name was well known in the championship. We had just won promotion to *Segunda* (the Spanish second division) and were looking for someone with experience at that level,' explains Gerardo Molina, then technical director of Racing Ferrol, a town buried in the north-west of Spain. The man in charge

---

3   Mourinho ended his playing career at 23 after unimpressive seasons with Rio Ave (where his father was coach), Belenenses and Sesimbra.

was a charismatic manager who favoured a very attacking game: Luis
Cesar Sampedro. 'He was a reference point for Unai, he often talked
about him,' recalls Iñaki Bea, who played with Emery a few years
later at Lorca. 'Luis Cesar believed in attacking football, with one
striker and a very high defensive line. He wanted to press high up the
pitch and win the ball in attack and then pass it around. It was never
easy to play against his sides.' The proof was that the club stayed up
without any problem (16th out of 22 teams) with the ninth highest
number of goals. Emery started in a third of the matches (he played
in 28 of the 42 championship games and started 14 times). 'He was
good technically, but he had no edge to him, no strong presence. He
found it hard to deal with pressure,' was Molina's view.

By now, Emery was coming up to 30 and still far from settled,
while always nearby were the ice packs and the tubes of Voltarène to
soothe his injured knee. 'To some extent, fear was always at the back
of my mind. I didn't know how to cope with it because nobody had
taught me to, and I wasn't able to do so on my own. A footballer who
doesn't want to play doesn't worry about that kind of thing when he
doesn't actually play. Not me.' Joking with his friends, he once told
them that he sometimes 'shat himself', adding more seriously that
'[my] footballing career was more painful than joyful.'

During his second season at Racing Ferrol, Unai got to know the
new boys, in particular the small group of Francophones brought
to the club by a young agent called Claude Cauvy. In autumn 2001,
Cauvy appeared on French TV in the *Seven Capital Sins* programme,
presented by Julien Courbet. This covered Cauvy's playing career,
which was said to be fake.[4] Among the new arrivals that summer
were Samir Boughanem, the Moroccan international midfielder,
and Philippe Burle, a defender from Ajaccio, followed by Mickaël
Marsiglia (ex-Marseille), Ludovic Delporte (ex-Lens) and the
globetrotter Kaba Diawara, who returned to Ferrol at the very end of

---

4   Cauvy gave his version of the story in his book *Le Tour du Monde en Ballon*, [*Around
the World with a Football*], subtitled *Pour ouvrir des yeux et fermer des gueules* [*To open eyes and shut
mouths*]. He says he played six months at Real Madrid, then at Barça (there is no record
of this in either of the clubs' archives) before embarking on a world tour that took in
Chile, Mexico and Iceland.

his career. 'It was the beginning of a tradition of French players. I did a bit of everything at the club, especially looking after the new players for anything and everything, like finding a locksmith when a player comes home late at night but has left his keys inside,' says Molina, the go-to man at Ferrol. 'I arrived here in 1977 as the assistant trainer. Eventually, I became the head coach, doctor, masseur, spokesman, technical director and manager […] I'm a *Racinguista* to my dying day. When things are going badly for the team, I suffer,' Molina told the *Correo Gallego* in 2009.

Fortunately for him, the 2001-02 season was pure pleasure. Ferrol won game after game and became a contender for the top spot thanks to its red-hot attack (58 goals, the second highest total behind the champions Atlético). 'We collapsed at the end of the season when we were in fourth or fifth place with five games to go,' Marsiglia remembers. 'We had a really interesting set-up, a very attacking 4-4-2. In midfield, I played alongside Nenad Grozdic, the former Lens player: it was great.' Eventually finishing ninth, *Los diablos verdes* (the Green Devils) lit up a town known before only as the birthplace of General Franco, and one where the progressive loss of industry has led to an exodus of its inhabitants (from 87,000 to 77,000 between 1980 and 2000, and only around 70,000 today). 'We could sense a real fervour all around us. It's a town in the shadow of La Coruña, I think that came into it as well. We were high up the table, playing great football, and that was a way of saying we existed too,' Marsiglia recalls.

In this euphoria, Emery had an excellent first campaign, even scoring some goals. The arrival of Ludovic Delporte, later nicknamed 'the Beckham of La Mancha', meant that Emery was like the joker in the pack, although he still played 33 matches, 17 of them from the start, scoring seven goals. 'He was the one who provided me with crosses! I scored any number of goals thanks to him. He had a great left foot, he served up great free-kicks. Well, he could have made a lot more decisive passes, because I missed quite a lot of them,' laughs Philippe Burle, delighted to be talking about Emery. 'I don't have memories of a lot of players, but I do of him. Probably because we were both crazy about football.' Despite leaving Spain in 2012 to begin a successful coaching career in Qatar and Oman, the images of the bars and bodegas of Ferrol immediately come back to him. 'We used to like to get together over a glass of wine: he was really fond of that! So was the coach. You would see him in the street or in a bar, he was never bothered what you were drinking. On the contrary, he would say: "Here you go, it's my round!"'

The coach, Luis Cesar Sampedro, was well-known in the *Segunda*, where he is still managing, with Lugo in Galicia. He is someone whose psychology has inspired several of his players to become managers, like Marsiglia and Burle. 'When I first joined the club, he looked after me,' says Burle. 'He took me off at half-time in my first game, I was dreadful. We were losing 0-1, in the end we won 2-1. The next match, against Tarragona, was called off after eighteen minutes due to rain. Unlike in France or England, we didn't have to replay the whole game, but started again a few days or weeks later from the eighteenth minute. We had been losing 0-2, and all the players were looking suspiciously at me... I'd had a bad first game, but Sampedro had put me on again, and it was partly my fault we were losing. The following day, I went to see the coach and he told me: "Don't worry, there's no problem, I trust you!" The next Sunday we were at home to Santander or Oviedo, I can't remember which. The local newspaper had a photo of me saying it would be my last match if I didn't perform. At half-time, the coach took me off again. I couldn't understand why, because I was having a great match... It was 0-0, but we went on to lose 0-2. So, the next day I went to see him: "I'm sorry, here I am again, I thought I had a good first-half but you took me off. You must have thought I wasn't playing well."'"Did you see today's papers?', he said.

'No, I haven't bought them yet.'

'Well, they've crucified me. Do you know why?'

'No.'

'Because I took you off. They say you were the best player on the pitch. I prefer them to crucify me rather than you. Above all, I didn't want you to make any mistakes in the second half, because now everybody knows you're a good player.'

'In the next match I played 90 minutes at Numancia, and we won 1-0. I thanked Sampedro because there aren't many people who would have done that. He supported my career in Spain and put my welfare above his own. That's the sign of a psychologist, a great manager.'

A great teacher, Sampedro always left the door to his office open to his players. 'Unai was in there a lot. He took a little notebook with him, and when he came out, he'd made notes,' says Marsiglia. Emery also completed his coaching certificates at La Coruña, travelling there all the time and sometimes spending the evening in the Galician capital to admire the local club, at that time nicknamed 'Super Depor'. 'I used to go to watch their matches, especially in the European Cup. Whenever I was in the stands, I would see Unai there too,' Sampedro says with a smile. 'We saw some mythical games in the Riazor: Milan, Manchester United, the famous 4-3 against Paris…' The Real Club Deportivo de la Coruña was at its peak (champions in 2000, runners-up in 2001 and 2002, winners of the Copa del Rey in 2002) with Jacques Songo'o, Mauro Silva, Roy Makaay, Victor, Djalminha and the incredible Fran.

'Unai is known for using wide players to attack, and he started doing that after seeing what Depor did. They had great players, a superb team and really used their wide men, which was very unusual at the time,' Benito explains. Analysing the game, the combinations or tactics became all-important for Emery. 'I wonder if he felt entirely a player?' says Molina. 'Obviously on one level he did, but unconsciously, perhaps not. During a game he would be on the bench and I've seen him giving players instructions, telling them where they should play!' This habit began back at Toledo, where Emery started studying for the basic training diploma. 'I was a sub and I would tell my teammates where they should be on the pitch. My coach, Miguel Angel Portugal, once turned to me and told me off because I was giving the orders rather than him,' he remembers.

In the summer 2002, Unai left Galicia for Leganés, a club in the south-west of Madrid, squeezed between Alcorcón and Getafe. The club was as ambitious as it was unstable, a common occurrence in the Spanish second division. Yet again, there were two managers that year, and the *Pepineros,* so-called because in the past the region was known for growing cucumbers, only stayed up thanks to the misfortunes of Compostela, who came ninth but were relegated because of non-payment of wages to the players and staff. Ironically, the Madrid team also escaped thanks to the apocalyptic season Ferrol had, which ended in relegation. 'It was a complicated season,' sighs Juan Carlos Carcedo, a player notably for Atlético Madrid and Nice. 'I got on with Unai from the outset. We didn't just like football, we wanted to know all the players in the opposing teams, and to talk tactics. We also studied a course on managing sporting enterprises together. We profited from being in Madrid to try to have a door open for when our playing careers ended. Deep down, we both knew this would have something to do with football.' The two men became friends, as did another teammate, Pablo Villa. Carcedo is Emery's long-time assistant, and Villa also later accompanied him to Seville and Paris. 'There are teammates you lose contact with, which is only normal. But with Unai, we really shared our passion, and our relationship went beyond Leganés and football.'

Playing in 29 games, Unai to some extent re-discovered the pleasures of regular football. His knee continued to trouble him, but he could still play well on the left-wing. 'Overall, he wasn't very strong, but he was good enough to send in early crosses for the striker. And he was quick on the ball, and knew how to position himself, and who to give the ball to,' Carcedo continues, adding mischievously: 'You never know during a player's career what will happen if he becomes a trainer. But it's a fact that Unai already had these concerns about the game, to know how to play against such and such a team, what system to adopt to counter an opponent [...] You can never know what direction life will take you, but both of us were impressed by that.'

3.2

INTERVIEW WITH LUIS CÉSAR SAMPEDRO

At the age of 50, Luis César Sampedro knows all the ins and outs of Spanish football. He first played as a goalkeeper for Racing de Ferrol, then became a coach there, followed by Tarragona, Ejido, Alcoyano, Albacete, Valladolid and Lugo, in the Spanish second division. For two years in Galicia, he was Unai's manager.

Unai as player

'He came out of a good footballing school, Real Sociedad, where the players learn the ideas of commitment, effort and dedication. I found him to be a passionate, generous player with a lot of talent. He was someone completely devoted to his sport, someone who really loved football. He played a great part in the team during his first season, and even in the second one until a Frenchman, Ludovic Delporte, arrived. Unai always behaved impeccably, I can't fault him in any way for his professionalism. When he was first choice, he always played his best. And when he didn't play so often, he always accepted it as a professional.'

Fear of pressure

[*Sampedro thinks for a moment*] 'Well, I wasn't inside his head, but the brain is constantly emitting images. Occasionally, those images dominate the way you react, and there are many things that can affect how well you do your job. There are even things that can undermine you, others that block your desire to perform well. This fear can lead to a mistake in a situation that a priori seemed easy for the player. But everyone copes as best they can, and Unai was always very responsible. Maybe at those moments, in those matches, it was his brain that got in the way of his playing ability.'

His coaching vocation

'In my years as a manager I've got to know many players. You can never imagine some of them becoming trainers, but that wasn't the case with Unai. I'll illustrate that with an anecdote. Every Monday after the weekend matches, he knew all the results from the *Liga*, *Segunda* or *Segunda B*, just as I did. Once, as we were warming-up, one of his teammates was talking about a game, and Unai corrected him, because he knew absolutely everything: if his former teammates had scored, who else had, etc. Early on Monday morning he would go and buy all the Spanish sporting press and then come to our training session as someone who had learnt his lesson.'

Sampedro's idea of football

'I think you have to enjoy whatever it is you do. If you pursue your work without passion or joy… *joder*! (shit!), there's something missing, isn't there? That's the first step towards doing things badly. […] I believe in a certain kind of football, a certain kind of player. I don't like playing mechanically or routinely, even if I don't have intrinsically wonderful players. I like the beautiful game, and to win obviously, but…. it's like food. Some people like a certain kind of cuisine, others don't. And, of course, you have to eat according to your budget. But what I don't understand is people who eat badly when they do have money. If you're rich and you still like to eat badly… Well, it's something similar when you're a trainer. If I have good players, I'm not going to play ugly football, or in a style I don't like. Yeah, I may win, but it's one thing to be effective, and another to get the most out of your players to produce football that wins and that the fans like.'

Transition from player to manager

'A lot of people think that being a player is like being a manager… they don't know what they're talking about. Of course, it can help, but a great player isn't necessarily a better trainer than a player who had a mediocre career. An example: a nurse can spend twenty years in an operating theatre with a surgeon who specializes in knee operations. That nurse can be excellent at her job, taking part in a thousand operations and helping the surgeon. That's fine, but she's never, in fact, carried out an operation. And it's the same for those people in football who believe they can become surgeons because they've been in the same theatre as trainers. A lot of people think they can be trainers, but they're two different professions, two different skill sets […] Unai has succeeded because he always wanted to learn. He researched, studied and doubtless came to the same conclusions as I did: you need to really love this sport and to understand that the key factor in today's football is the mental side, the psychology. I don't mean for the stars, like Modric or Iniesta, more for your average player. It's the brain that dominates, and the images it transmits can undermine all the good work done up till then – and so trainers have to be aware of the power of the mind, because it's decisive in the balance between success or failure.

'Even ten years ago, some trainers in Spain were a disaster. They knew nothing about tactics, so if you were better than them at that, you could always get by. That's no longer the case. All the managers have a good knowledge of tactics, and a competent staff behind them to help prepare the players. It's not like it used to be, when some of them sent out their players to run around and fight. Nowadays, it's psychology that makes the difference between trainers. If Unai has been so successful, it's because he's understood that for years, probably as a result of his own weaknesses as a player.'

4

TEMPLE OF THE SUN

To travel south down Spain's east coast can seem monotonous. Crossing Catalonia, Valencia with its endless detours and then the huge resorts of the Costa Blanca (Calpe, Benidorm…) offers few surprises. So why venture even further south? Beautiful Andalusia is still 200 kilometres away, and to get there you have to pass through Murcia, one of those places nobody ever really visits, unless it's to get a suntan at the Manga del Mar Menor. Murcia is the Cinderella province, left out of tourist brochures and government plans. Nobody seems concerned about it, even if food-lovers like to order an *ensalada murciana* (tomatoes, boiled egg, onion, tuna, black olives and olive oil) in restaurants in Madrid or Navarre. Spain tends to look the other way. As a country, it prefers not to see Murcia's lunar landscape, treating it almost as if it was invisible. Perhaps it's because of the dry dust that stings your face, or the blindingly white horizon. Even if all that is true, it's no reason to think Lorca only exists in school textbooks. 'Earth is probably the lost paradise,' one of Spain's greatest poets wrote, as a metaphor for the town that bears his name, even though he wasn't born there. It was to Lorca that Emery came in the summer of 2003, to a club then in *Segunda B*: Lorca Deportiva Club de Futbol.

When talking of football and Lorca, you have to be careful: Lorca Deportiva replaced Lorca CF, which folded in 2002, and in 1994 Lorca CF had already replaced the extinct Club de Futbol Lorca Deportiva. What's in a name? It seems as if football clubs

in Lorca die young. As if that weren't enough, a Lorca Atletico
Club de Futbol existed from 1996 to 2012, and another club, La
Hoya Lorca Club de Futbol, was created in 2003. Today this is
owned by the former Chinese international Xu Genbao and enjoys
the nickname of *'El Brocoli Mecanico'* ('the Clockwork Broccoli').[5]
It's all a big puzzle, especially considering that the town of Lorca has little
more than 90,000 inhabitants… At the Lorca Deportiva Club de Futbol,
a local man was in charge: Pedro Reverte, only 27 years old. 'Unai was a
left-sided player with a good playing record and good technique. What I
wanted was to put together a competitive team with very skilled players.
I thought he would fit in well, like other Basque footballers,' explains
Reverte. Among the many Basques he signed were Iñaki Bea, a
defender playing in the lower divisions, most recently for the nearby
CF Ciudad de Murcia. 'I roomed with Unai… He's someone who…
[he pauses]. Some players like dogs, others like video games, travel,
women or stocks and shares. But the only thing Unai ever talked about
was football.' This view is seconded by Xavier Moro, a French-Spanish
midfielder born in Paris who played for Barça as a youngster. 'With
your teammates you talk about your family, your friends, or maybe
about music. But with Unai, whenever we had a coffee together,
we always talked football, tactics or about players we had seen.'
So, Emery was lucky: he fell in with a group that was as crazy about
football as he was. 'We had a real understanding, and that spread to the
pitch,' confirms Moro.

At the end of the season, the club was in second place for the
play-offs for promotion to the Spanish second division. Put like that,
it sounds simple: home and away games for the semi-final, then a final
to decide who wins the big prize. Except that, contrary to what looks
like common sense and what is common practice in all the play-offs
throughout the world, the labyrinths of Spanish football seem to have
been created by some kind of mad genius. So, you come top in one of
the four sections in *Segunda B*? You don't get automatically promoted,
but you are at the head of a pool of the top four teams from each of

---

5   In 2013, for the club's second season, the team strip was designed to look like broccoli. This was meant to be in honour of the vegetable grown extensively around Lorca,
especially on land owned by several of the club's directors.

the sections who play each other twice. At the end of these six games, the winner of each mini-championship is promoted to the *Segunda*.[6]

'We were on track right up to the final game. We had to travel to Pontevedra: the winner would win promotion,' recalls Bea. About 16,000 fans crammed into a stadium supposed to hold a maximum 12,000. Driven on, the club from Galicia beat Lorca with two goals from 'Rifle' Javier Rodriguez, who ironically two years later played for Lorca. Emery, who played the whole game, ended up flat out on the pitch, secretly promising himself he would never experience that feeling again.

In the 2004-05 season, Lorca became even more ambitious, openly aiming for promotion. 'Except that, from being the pleasant surprise of the previous year, now we were one of the favourites, which made it very difficult for us in the opening months,' says Bea. There began to be questions about the methods employed by the trainer Quique Yagüe. 'He was very old school,' according to several of the players, even though they admitted they respected him for helping win promotion from the *Tercera*. Pedro Reverte, at that time the club's sporting director, felt that he had to change something. 'We wanted to compete for promotion, but at Christmas we were mid-table. We needed to make a change in the dressing room, in every sense.'

The club president, Antonio Baños Albacete, called Reverte into his office. 'We quickly came to the conclusion that the best thing for the club was a change in the dugout. I told him that in my view the new trainer should be Unai Emery. Although at first he looked at me as if I was mad, he backed me up. Why Unai? He already had his coach's diplomas – not just levels one and two but also three, the top level. When he was injured, he always asked me if he could accompany me to the games. I heard him assessing certain things and was often surprised about how well he grasped every aspect of the game, even though he was only a player. He was cut out to be a coach, he stored

6   Apparently considering this wasn't complicated enough, the organisers later dreamt up a 'route of champions' as well as a 'route of non-champions' where in the second round, the teams losing the semi-finals of the 'route of champions' re-appear. In short: don't ever get relegated to the Spanish third division. Make sure you stay in the second.

everything away in his memory. It's funny: I remember I used to watch him all the time, and he always found a solution to the problem we were facing on the pitch.' It remained to be seen whether Unai would accept, because he often had to struggle with his fear of disappointing, to the extent that he always anxiously looked up the match rating he was given in the football newspaper *Marca*. 'I sat him down in my office and asked him: "Would you be scared if I told you I want you to be the coach?" the former president of the club later told Roberto Arrocha, a famous journalist for the *ABC* newspaper, based in Seville. 'Do you know what he replied? "Not at all. If that's what you want, I'll be your coach." He was so sure of himself it made my decision easier. Several days went by and the trainer Quique Yagüe, who I was already getting fed up with, yet again put out a defensive team. I told Pedro: "Call Unai." I knew he wouldn't disappoint me.'

In the meantime, Emery got in touch with a few friends to ask their advice. 'I was in Colombia for the South American Under-20s tournament. Alberto Benito was with me. Unai called him so that he would ask me if I thought he could be a coach and continue playing. I told him that in my opinion it was impossible,' says Mikel Etxarri, his former mentor. He adds: 'When he was playing for Toledo I think, he called me to ask for some of my notes because he said Alberto Benito was studying for his training diploma. I knew that, in fact, it was for him.'

Unai Emery was 34 years old, with a smashed knee that meant he only played five games, mostly on the left-wing. 'It's a story he has often told on *Radio Marca*. During his last match, I teased him,' laughs teammate Xavier Moro, 'He really wanted to play but he wasn't fit. I looked at him and said: "Unai, if you're injured, now's the moment to tell the coach!" That was the last time he played. He lasted the first half, but after that never appeared on the pitch,' says Moro. A final visit to the doctor convinced Emery to quit his first love. 'The doctor told me that if I insisted on playing, I could have mobility problems in the long term. In short, that was the end of it as far as hoping to play at that level was concerned. So I threw myself into being a trainer, without too many regrets. That was what I wanted to do.'

In order to give them the news, Pedro Reverte brought together the experienced players in the team. They were surprised, shocked even.

'We were all taken by surprise, because none of us thought of him as a coach,' says Juan Carlos Ramos, a striker from Seville who has played for many clubs in southern Spain. 'It wasn't exactly unheard of, but it wasn't normal either. We left for our Christmas break saying goodbye to our teammate, a lad we got changed and had a shower with. When we got back, he was our coach. But to be frank it all went smoothly right from the start. Our group was professional enough to see the difference between Unai as our teammate and Unai the trainer.' Better still, his appointment acted as a stimulus for some of the players. 'Every time the coach changes there's a reaction in the dressing room. The first training sessions are more intense because there's a new deal. And Emery brought a new spirit, the new motivation we needed. Our previous trainer maybe no longer shared the same passion as the players. When Unai came in, he began to use videos, to change tactics, to make sure our training sessions were more varied. Before that, our coach really was old-fashioned, so the change renewed our strength, enthusiasm, our passion for football,' according to Bea. Now Unai had to translate that enthusiasm into results.

On Saturday 8 January 2005, Unai boarded the team coach as their trainer for the first time. According to club president Albacete in his interview with *ABC*, nothing seemed to have changed: 'He kept his head down the whole time. He started reading and carried on doing so. Wow! Maybe he was in a funk. I think, in fact, he was studying the other team's players or reading something about tactics and strategies. *Que tío!*' The temple of the sun was almost 400 kilometres away: Ecija, a town in the province of Seville affectionately known as *'La sartén de Andalucía'*, literally the Andalusian frying-pan, so named because of the excessive summer heat. Somewhere said to pardon no one, especially those who aren't ready to enter hell. 'I can remember everything perfectly: the trip, the hotel, going out onto the field, the line-up… we were ready,' Emery told the Murcia newspaper *La Verdad* in 2009.

Sunday 9 January 2005, Écija Balompié v. Lorca Deportiva Club de Futbol was about to kick-off. The two teams ran out onto the pitch to an unexpected cool breeze. The Estadio San Pedro was silent, only half-full. Unai Emery looked all round him. Deep down, he knew it was the start of a new life.

5

A PROPHET IN HIS OWN LAND

Iñaki Bea has a good memory. More than ten years have passed, but that game against Ecija is still vivid in his mind. 'I was in the starting line-up. After a quarter of an hour we scored a goal from a throw-in based on a move we had practised on the training ground. We realised at once that we were on the right track, what the boss wanted was being reflected on the pitch. In the end we won 3-0 thanks to his new approach. We all said to each other in the changing-room: "Shit, we're a different team!" It wasn't the team of the week before that came to train and collect its salary, win or lose.' Juan Carlos Ramos, who scored late on in the game, goes further: 'Unai succeeded in transmitting his love of football that perhaps we had lost. That was the basis of what he told us, and what made us believe in his ideas, his way of working. I'll be frank: I wasn't always in the starting line-up, but I loved playing for him. I'm an attacking player and he gave me a great deal of freedom. He also listened to me: we could discuss the impressions we had, which isn't something I've found with all my coaches…'

Lorca rapidly moved towards the top of the table with what was a seductive, even revolutionary game for the time and for *Segunda B*. 'We could be playing away from home or against one of the favourites, Unai didn't care. He focused completely on winning and scoring goals. So we had some famous victories', says Moro, referring to the 7-1

against Díter Zafra and the 5-0 against Marbella, a promotion rival.
More than the attacking players, it was the way Lorca recovered the
ball that amazed people. 'We had four or five moves that we did at top
speed, because we could dominate all the other teams with our pressing
tactics. We kept a high defensive line which led to lots of offsides,'
says Bea, a rock in central defence. 'I improved a lot tactically: when
to step forward to catch their forward offside, when to intercept...
I've never been very quick, so I was a bit nervous at the start. I
gradually gained in confidence. I told myself: "Shit, I may be slow,
but I'm forty or fifty metres from my own goal!" Thanks to Unai I
learned to think on a football pitch.'

Lorca's crazy gallop up the table created an unprecedented
fervour in the town. Most delighted of all was Pedro Reverte, the
man who signed Unai as a player and then convinced the president
he would make an ideal trainer. 'I was born here, and to see that the
club could arouse such passion... When I come back here or talk to
any of the locals, they always remember that time.' In the following
months, the thousand or so lost souls who regularly turned up at
the Estadio Francisco Artés Carras (named after the president of
the Club Deportivo Lorca in the 1950s) were joined by many more:
a welcome sight in a stadium with a capacity of more than 8,000
fans that had been inaugurated on 5 March 2003 with a friendly
against Barça. 'Beyond the sporting achievement, it was the human
aspect that people remember from that season,' says Xavier Moro.
'Unai is an honest guy. He was always sincere with us. He would use
a metaphor from life outside football, telling us that you have to
help the new generations, that a family grows with love. And it's the
same with a football club. You have to love your sport, stay honest
and help one another. He encouraged that feeling, and was lucky
because we were a healthy team, willing to listen.'

Creating the right state of mind: Emery understood that perfectly,
even though he was learning the job without any real experience. 'After
my playing career, I became part of the staff at Levante,' says Iñaki
Bea. 'I sometimes asked myself if I was ready to manage a team in
Segunda B. Honestly, I don't think I was. Nowadays I'm the assistant

coach at Eibar and I've learnt from the head coach and from all my experience on the bench, so I think I could do it. That's what was crazy about Unai. How could he be so good with his choices and his psychology when he had been a player only a couple of weeks earlier?' Bea goes on: 'When I'm travelling in my car, I often ask myself questions. The other day I was wondering how a novice teacher could stand up in front of a class and teach a subject. Wouldn't it be better for him to spend five or six months learning as an assistant? To go into the class, listen to the teacher and learn how to deal with the students: that would be bound to enrich him.' A teacher? Unai already looked like one: a pair of small glasses, a notebook always stuffed in his pocket, and wearing the club sweater, often beneath a grey or black tracksuit. 'Yes, a teacher, it's a good comparison,' the Basque footballer agrees. 'You could ask every Lorca player and I'm sure they would all say they learnt something from Unai.'

Sunday 22 May 2005: the last game but one in the *Segunda B* season. Lorca were fifth with 55 points, only one behind Marbella, who were in fourth and looked certain to qualify for the play-offs. Marbella were playing an early game away to Extremadura, a team in mid-table. Defying all logic, the locals thrashed the team from Andalusia 4-0. By the time they went out onto the pitch, Emery's team knew they could finally get into the top four, something they had dreamed of since the previous September. Since fate is fond of sweet irony, this crucial game was against... Ecija, who they hammered 6-0. 'From the moment he took over the team, Unai never stopped being positive. He was convinced we could win promotion,' says Ramos, in the starting line-up for the last game, a 2-1 victory at Jaén that guaranteed Lorca fourth place. As a bonus, Lorca finished with the highest number of goals in the four *Seguna B* groups, together with Alicante, the undisputed champion in its pool, and Lorca's first opponent in the play-offs.

That year there was no mini-championship to reach *Segunda,* simply a semi-final and then a final played home and away. Lorca took this in their stride, beating Alicante 1-0 at home, and then 2-1 in the Estadio José Rico Perez, the biggest stadium in Alicante specially taken over for the game. Strangely, it was one of the usual substitutes, Jorge Perona, who scored in both games. 'That was one of our team's strong points,' says Bea. 'Unai managed to keep the players who didn't play for long focused. He looked after them, and that made them happy.'

Emery was going to need all his players for the final, against a team desperately trying to regain its past glory... the Real Unión Club of Irun. 'It was like coming home. A really strong symbol. Irun is right next to our village: that's where our grandfather and father played. All our family was going to be there,' Igor Emery explains.

Sunday 19 June 2005: the Estadio Francisco Artés Carras looked full for the first time since the friendly against Barcelona. The press cuttings speak of 7,000 spectators, something unthinkable only a few months earlier according to Pedro Reverte: 'I think a lot of fans were pleased and touched to be part of this achievement. Two years earlier we had been in *Tercera*, and now...' It has to be said that ever since January, Lorca had been admired by all the other teams. 'We were being paid properly and on time, a good wage compared to the average Spanish worker, but less than most of the players in the other clubs. But money isn't everything, is it?' says Xavier Moro, who was suspended for the crucial match. He did though join in the festive atmosphere in the town, where the *peñas lorquinas*[7] organised the 'promotion caravan', a huge procession with banners, chants and visits to bars, with everybody wearing the club's blue and white colours. Unfortunately, Irun hadn't just come for the party – in the previous round had knocked out the favourites, Rayo Vallecano. Against Lorca, although Perona equalised at the start of the second half, Real Unión ended up winning 2-1. 'After all our efforts, the incredible rise up the table, that was perhaps the only match we didn't give everything,' remembers Ramos, who was as ineffective up front as Iñaki Bea was in defence. 'To lose at home... We were all discouraged, and not many thought we could recover.' 'It was tough coming in on that Monday, but Unai took us all down to the beach to train.' This decision was taken together with Pedro Reverte, suffering

---

7   *Peñas* are groups of fans. There are thousands of them throughout Spain.

in the stands with the others that Sunday. 'I'll never forget that day. I'll never forget that defeat. Everyone was depressed. After that game, it seemed impossible we would win promotion. [...] We went down to Aguilas, a wonderful village on the coast. The boss wanted all the players and staff to come back from there convinced we were going up, and that's what happened. It was there that we really won promotion.' No doubt poets would have been charmed by the idea of meeting on one of those enchanting beaches, especially García Lorca, who wrote: 'The most terrible of all emotions is that of the death of hope.' He needn't have worried: hope won't die for anyone who really opens their eyes on the playa Poniente.

***

Sunday 26 June 2005: Irun. The whole Emery family made the six-kilometre journey from Hondarribia. That morning, the Lorca team saw a bus already decked out to celebrate Irun's promotion. 'That annoyed my brother, and he used it as extra motivation,' says Igor, who commentated the game for the local Gipuzkoa radio. At one o'clock, shortly before lunch, Unai went to talk to Juan Carlos Ramos. 'He told me I wasn't going to start the game, but that he was counting on me at some point in the match. I was starting regularly, and at a moment like that, when everybody is keen to play... soon afterwards my dad called me and said "Don't worry, I know you're going to come on and score the winning goal." I told him I didn't think it was going to happen, because I'd been lucky enough to do that with Cordoba a few years earlier (in 1999) and there was no way it could happen again.'

For his part, Moro had been brought back to make the midfield more mobile. 'But in the warm-up, I picked up an injury. I knew I had but clenched my teeth and said nothing.' He went back sadly to the changing-room, hearing the deafening chants of the fans in the Stadium Gal, where according to the reports 8,000 people were crammed into a ground with a supposed maximum capacity of 6,344. The Lorca team was the first out onto the pitch in their dark blue

shirts. Then it was the turn of the home team, received with a storm
of applause, confetti and streamers. This premature celebration only
increased the fears in Lorca at the far end of the country, where a
giant screen had been put up in the Recinto Ferial de Santa Quiteria,
which has since been demolished.

Even local people who didn't follow football turned up to watch.
'I don't like football, but I was there, jumping up and down in my
dressing-gown and slippers so that my husband wouldn't be on
his own in that joyous fiesta,' wrote a certain Carmen Ruiz several
days later in the letters page of *La Verdad* newspaper. She and her
husband were able to shout with joy just before half-time, following
a short corner and a cross and a header from Jorge Sánchez, a striker
described by Bea as 'busy, hard-working and with an aggressive
edge that was perhaps missing in others like Ramos'. That made the
score Real Unión Club 0-Lorca Deportiva Club de Fútbol 1 (2-2 on
aggregate). The goal only added to the tension already felt by Juan
Emery, who was in the stands. 'Our dad was suffering so badly he
decided to leave at half-time. He couldn't bear it anymore. He left
and walked all the way home to Hondarribia! And apart from the
match, there was also a festival in Irun,' remembers Igor, who also
interviewed his brother.

At the start of the second half the visitors were still dominant,
winning free-kick after free-kick. In the 53rd minute, from one of
these almost 30 metres out and slightly to the left of centre, Jorge
Perona decided to go for goal. In his youth, he had been a prolific
scorer for his age group with Barça and the Spanish national under-
16s. Now aged 22, he seemed to rediscover his youthful success and
scored with a vicious shot that went in off the post. 'He's left me
speechless,' shouted one of the presenters for the local TV station in
Murcia. Real Unión Club 0-Lorca Deportiva Club de Fútbol 2 (2-3
on aggregate). The minutes went slowly by. Emery paced up and
down, put on his three substitutes. Already on 30 minutes he had
been forced to replace the injured Huegun with Sergi Mesa, a stockily
built striker. Mesa in turn was replaced on the hour mark by Xabier
Sánchez, a midfielder who collected 134 yellow and nine red cards

during his playing career. Then, with 15 minutes to go, Juan Carlos
Ramos came on the field. By now Irun were playing long balls up to
their strikers, but without success. Unai was still pacing in the technical
area. The five minutes of stoppage time were full of scrappy play
and more long balls. In the final minute, Irun's veteran Egoitz Sukia
miraculously took the ball on the six-metre line and sent the game into
extra time. As Moro remembers: 'When he scored like that, in the dying
seconds... "Shit," I said to myself, "couldn't you have done it earlier,
to give us the chance to score?"' At the end of 90 minutes it was Real
Unión Club 1-Lorca Deportiva Club de Fútbol 2 (3-3 on aggregate).
Unai Emery went out onto the pitch to encourage his players: 'I've
always thought that there's a hope of winning every match as long as
it's not all over.' But then it was straight on to extra-time.

After little more than a minute, it seemed as if fate had already
come down on one side. 'I'd already been booked, so the ref had his
eye on me,' says Iñaki Bea, annoyed because his clearance had hit his
hand and fallen at Sukia's feet for him to score. 'Now in extra time I
stumbled and collided with their goalkeeper. The ref thought I was
trying to obstruct him, so he sent me off.' It seemed as though the
sky was about to fall in on the Lorca players. Fortunately, it stayed
above them, though they were suffering from cramp and aching
muscles. 'By now our team was really struggling, with players who
were weary and even injured still on the field...' says Juan Carlos
Ramos, catching his breath. 'I can still remember it well. Irun were
pressing and pressing, and we were suffering. Then came that move
in the second half of extra-time.'

Antonio Robles, the Lorca captain, was defending high up the
pitch. He recovered the ball close to the halfway line, on his right.
Ramos was in front of him, about 40 metres from the Irun goal.
Robles slipped the ball to his striker. 'My first reaction was to look
up,' remembers Ramos. 'I saw the goalie was out of his goal, so I
shot...' Everyone in the stadium followed the path of the ball as
it flew through the air. 'We looked at each other and we knew. We
knew as soon as he took the shot. We knew because he'd already
scored a goal like that the same year,' says Moro. It was a perfect

lob, and it silenced the locals. On the right-hand side of the ground, all the members of the Lorca dugout raced onto the pitch, Emery ahead of all the others, jumping for joy. The presenters on Murcia TV went crazy, repeating '*Goal! goal! goal!*' more than 45 times. Even Igor Emery was beside himself. 'It wasn't easy to stay calm, especially when I saw my brother leaping round the pitch like a madman!'

There were still nine minutes left to play, but that didn't matter: as so often happens in the Basque country, the rain had suddenly started to lash down, Irun couldn't find a way back, and Lorca was promoted to the second division. Igor recalls: 'I hugged my brother when the final whistle went. It was the start of something for him, for all of us. The whole family ate with the team after the match, to share the moment...'

Real Unión Club 1-Lorca Deportiva Club de Fútbol 3 (3-4 on aggregate).

More than 12 years have gone by since then, but Unai still remembers it clearly: 'It was incredible to find myself there, in the club where my father and grandfather had played... That goal was the strongest emotion I've ever felt in all my career. It was at the start of my career as a manager, but it was personal as well, something beyond football.'

6

EARTHQUAKE IN THE SECOND DIVISION

Spanish nights out are well-known for carrying on until dawn. This is a way of justifying the *siesta*, that delicious invention so common in the south of the country that, for many, is a way of celebrating life or good fortune. On the morning of 27 June 2005, Lorca was still celebrating: some people hadn't slept, others hadn't woken up; each bar had its own story to tell. The regional newspaper *La Verdad* illustrated the events of that crazy night with testimonies from local people who had watched the game on the giant screen or on their own TV sets. 'When they scored against us, I punched the TV and broke it. I had to watch the end of the match at a neighbour's,' someone called Antonio Gonzalez told the newspaper. Equally carried away was Joaquin Sanchez: 'I chewed all my fingernails down, but not my toenails, because I couldn't reach them, and anyway I was wearing slippers...'

Fifteen thousand people came out into the streets of Lorca to welcome back the 'heroes of Irun', an enthusiasm out of all proportion to the 25 fans who had braved the 900-kilometre journey between Lorca and the Basque country that Sunday. Emery was in the thick of the celebrations, but he was already thinking about the next season. 'The financial resources were very modest, but Unai created a squad with a well-defined identity. He knew perfectly well what was needed, although other people had doubts. Few of them were

confident about the future,' recalls Pedro Reverte. With a budget of
a little less than 350,000 euros, he obviously could not hope to sign
any big names. 'Normally, when a team wins promotion, the manager
wants to bring in new players who have experience of that division.
But Unai didn't do that. He kept the basis of the squad the same,
bringing in other players from *Segunda B*', explains Bea, spending no
more than 60,000 euros on transfers.[8] This came as no surprise to
those who knew him. 'He's always been interested in every division.
He knows all the players in the *Liga*, the *Segunda* and the *Segunda
B*. It's his passion, but it's also something that has helped him as
a manager,' according to his former teammate Alberto Benito. 'It's
not always easy to follow what's going on in *Segunda B*, but Unai
knew everything about it. All his former teammates, the managers,
the stadiums. It's a good job he has an excellent memory!'

Of course, several other players joined the squad, some with wide
experience, especially the Argentine player Facundo Sava, who was
under contract with Fulham, then in the English Premier League.
This was a masterstroke by Reverte, as Emery told *As:* 'We had our
eye on him at Celta (in the Spanish second division) and liked what
we saw. He was on loan from Fulham, where his contract still had a
year to run. We talked to his English club and managed to sign him by
paying only 20 per cent of his wages.' Sava was one of eight players
aged over 30 in the team, the majority of whom had never played any
higher than at the Spanish third level. 'Unai made us feel so confident
that we went into every match without fear. We started out with a
very attacking 4-3-3, with wide players who were encouraged to go
forward and get involved,' Bea remembers proudly. Moro agrees: 'We
were really good on the ball. The hardest thing when you go up a
division is to win respect from everyone: the managers, opposing
players, the media. In the end, we were always on TV because our
games were so entertaining. We often used to eat together after our
training sessions and used to joke: "If someone had told us that

---

8   'We spent 60,000 euros on Gorka De Carlos from Real Unión and Maldonado from
Ceuta. His contract was with Betis, so we had to negotiate.' Unai Emery to the sports
daily *AS*, on 12 March 2006.

almost thirty of our games would be televised, we'd have told the guy he was cracked!" We had a great time, as well as doing our jobs as well as possible.'

This enjoyment involved the whole group. 'Unai often told the young players: "Why don't you go out and enjoy yourselves!" Sometimes he would give us one or two days off, and when we ate together he wanted us to enjoy our meal, but to keep in mind that we had training the following day,' the Basque defender recalls. 'He always encouraged us to meet up together. But seeing he was now the manager, he couldn't do what he used to do as a player. When we went out for a beer, he would leave us after the second one, to allow us our own space. He no longer drank four or five with us […] And he knew each of us very well. He knew who was single, who was married, who liked to go out, who he could share a beer with. Part of a manager's job is psychological, making choices. For example, he didn't care if you were his friend, because that wouldn't help you play better. But on the other hand, if he put you on the bench, that didn't mean you weren't his friend anymore either. He was very good at handling all that.'

Emery handled his squad so well that Lorca could dream of going up to the *Liga* thanks to an incredible second half of the season and an explosive attack (56 goals, the third highest in the division). 'All through the season, Unai told us to believe in ourselves. He persuaded us to have greater self-belief,' says Ramos, who was the link player between midfield and the forwards, led by Facundo Sava. 'He was big and kept the ball very well, which brought our attack to life. Besides that, Facundo was a great guy. We know that all Argentines are passionate about football, but he was really crazy about it, even in the training sessions. He gave so much of himself that for him it wasn't training, it was a competition! And that spirit was catching.'

In addition to his footballing talents, Facundo Sava was the perfect match for Unai, according to Iñaki Bea. 'He had studied psychology, and I'm sure Unai learnt from him. I think they gave each other a lot, it was reciprocal.' The Argentine striker, known as *'El Colorado'*, was also passionate about reading, and shared his enthusiasm with other players like Moro: 'We used to swap books, because we had more or less the same tastes. But we also talked a lot about football. When you're lucky enough to have teammates who are really into football, that's all you need to achieve your aims.'

The aim of staying up was quickly achieved. Then Lorca could pursue another, more secret one: to win promotion to *La Liga*. This gentle madness that soon made headlines in the regional and national press. Both *Marca* and *AS* published many articles about the team and its young manager. He was even interviewed at length, with the eloquent heading: 'It's football that's beautiful, not the landscape or cars or women.' In Lorca, the excitement was plain to see: almost 2,000 local fans travelled to the game against the neighbouring club, Real Murcia. 'I've always thought that football has to be a pleasure. When I enter a stadium, I want my players to enjoy it, as well as all the spectators. And selfishly, I want to enjoy it myself, I want to feel the passion. From Lorca to now, I've always had that same wish,' says Unai.

A wish that was even stronger for the last three games of the season, with a miracle still possible. Lorca began this critical period playing at home to Lleida, who ended up being relegated. Nervous, untidy, Lorca lost 1-2 at the death. Far more important was the next match, against Levante, because both teams were hoping for third place behind Huelva and Tarragona. On 11 June 2006, around 1,800 *lorquinos* travelled to Valencia to help fill the stadium (close to 23,000 fans altogether). Just before half-time, Facundo Sava stepped up to take a penalty after a handball by the experienced Alexis Suarez. The Argentine was facing a fellow countryman in Pablo Cavallero, a former international. Cava side-footed the ball well with his left foot, but the goalkeeper just managed to get his fingertips to it and push it round the post. Sava buried his head in his hands while the Estadio Ciudad de Valencia went wild. Lorca had missed its chance and didn't get another one. The match ended 0-0. Levante went on to finish third, and Lorca fifth after a draw in their final game against Poli Ejido. 'That was an unforgettable year. Unai brought out the best in every player,' Reverte says admiringly. He is backed up by Xavi Moro: 'I've had a lot of managers during my career, but Unai... just talking about it makes my hair stand on end. He was perhaps the one who best understood and accepted me. It's more than ten years since then, but I don't need to see old videos of it to remember all we lived through, all we did… Unai has always given equal value to the player who recovers the ball as to the one who begins a move, or the person who scores. Maybe that season his values of hard work, sacrifice and solidarity were our reward. Unai was the boss, our boss, but he was open-minded […] One day we landed at Tenerife for a game and I said to him: "Tomorrow we have to play that corner with Ramos taking it." By that corner, I meant a move with two players on the near post, two on the far post, and myself on the penalty spot. Unai looked at me, a bit surprised:

"Are you sure?" he asked.

"Yes, I'm certain."

"OK, we'll do it then."

On the morning of the match, he got us together for the team talk and among the moves from set pieces he mentioned that kind of corner, which we hadn't really been practising for two months. What's amazing is that Ramos took it, and I scored! It's just a little anecdote to illustrate how he trusts people and the fact that he brings out all your best qualities while not forgetting your weaknesses.'

Walking round the centre of Lorca, famous for its baroque architecture, these football memories seem a long way off. Lorca Deportiva Club de Fútbol went out of existence in February 2015, stuck in *Tercera* and riddled with debt.[9] It has to be said that when Unai Emery moved on, the club was immediately relegated. 'Unai is a great professional, with whom I, and the entire club, were lucky enough to work,' says Pedro Reverte, nowadays in charge of the sporting area of the UCAM Murcia Club de Fútbol (currently in the third division). He knows better than anyone the feat achieved by Emery and his squad.

Lorca isn't a town that attracts visitors: in summer it's an oven, and its economy has never adapted to modern life. Studies by the AIS Group has the *ciudad del sol* in third place among Spanish towns of more than 50,000 inhabitants with the highest risk of being poor

---

9   However, another *Club de Fútbol Lorca Deportiva* has existed since 2012.

– 38.3 per cent of the population in 2015. Of course, agriculture still allows many families to survive, but at what cost? Its ground water levels are shrinking dangerously, something sadly now common in the south of Spain. Except that the Andalusian provinces with the same concerns (Almería and Huelva) don't run the same risk of earthquakes. Researchers have linked the lowering of the water table to the latest tremors. On 29 January 2005, an earthquake measuring 4.6 on the Richter scale struck the town, without causing any deaths. Six years later, on 11 May 2011, another earthquake of 5.1 on the scale did result in nine deaths, with another 324 unfortunate victims injured. The chief cause isn't that the underground water is over-exploited, but that is a contributing factor. It's a sad panorama, but in Lorca nobody complains. A walk round its neighbourhoods sees only smiles, each one brighter than the previous one. When the talk turns to football, it's Unai Emery's name that comes up, time and again. This makes Pedro Reverte, a true *Lorquino*, very happy. He adds as a final thought: 'Only Unai and I know how hard we worked and enjoyed those moments. *"Gracias por todo, compañero!"*'

7

THE GOOD, THE BAD AND THE UGLY

'My dream was simply to play for one of the teams in Almería province. I was born here, in Zapillo, a modest neighbourhood where I played football like all the other kids. To reach *La Liga* and make a living from football seemed far too distant for me...' José Ortiz Bernal pauses for a moment. The former captain of Unión Deportiva Almería has always been modest in the best sense of the term, not to build himself up later on. 'He's beyond reproach as a person,' all his former teammates agree. Nowadays the manager of two Dolores Promesas boutiques, one in Almería and the other in Málaga, he's very relaxed as he talks to me in the second of these. 'I finished my playing career in 2012 and started to go in for the triathlon. I'm okay on a bike, and the running allows me to catch up for the time I lose at the swimming. Before I took up the sport, I didn't exactly drown but I didn't really know how to swim either.' Almost a disgrace for someone from Almería, where the town and its beaches – especially those at Roquetas de Mar where Bernal lived and played – are right on the Mediterranean coast.

Our conversation quickly turns to Emery, who arrived there in 2006 after making a splash at his first club, Lorca, only 150 kilometres away. 'They were a really difficult team to play. They even finished higher than us when Unai was down there,' he continues, echoing what the winger Bruno Saltor told me. 'It was never a pleasure trip. The heat was stifling, and they pressed and pressed you. Nobody was expecting it, but Unai almost got them up into *La Liga*...' He received several offers, but Emery chose Almería, a town where the team was desperately awaiting a return to *La Liga* after a brief stay from 1979 to 1981. 'The problem was that a lot of clubs went bust. After the Agrupación Deportiva Almería disappeared, there wasn't one single club that represented the town. We had both the Polideportivo Almería and the Almería Club de Fútbol, which meant the fan base was split. There were only about 500 supporters for each team's games,' says Ortiz, who signed for Almería Club de Fútbol in 1997 while still studying to become a PE teacher. Apart from a six-month parenthesis with Ravenna in Italy (in *Serie B*), he stayed with the same team, which by then had become UD Almería.[10] 'Little by little, the club grew. It always had the ambition of returning to the highest level. For someone from Almería like me, the wait to get back into *La Liga* was starting to become far too long,' adds Francisco Rodríguez, the top goalscorer in the UDA's short history.

This ambition was enough to persuade Unai to offer a two-year contract to a certain Juan Carlos Carcedo, his former teammate from Leganés: 'He had already called me when he was at Lorca to see if I wanted to join him as his assistant. I couldn't go because I was already on the staff at Las Palmas, which meant that Almería was the first time we worked together. It was a very different context for both him and me. The club wanted promotion, and there was a lot of pressure. It wasn't the same as Lorca, and that helped Unai progress.'

Another former teammate joined them in Andalusia: Roberto Olabe.

'We were together at Real Sociedad, without being real friends; our friendship came later on, when we worked together. Having said that, there's an amusing detail, because when I had an injured shoulder, Unai had become closer to me, which says a lot about him [...] A few months before he came to Almería he had asked if we could work together in the future. And bizarrely, we both signed here at more or less the same time.'

From the start, Emery took the staff by surprise. They had been used to the ways of Paco Flores, previously the manager of Espanyol

---

10 When *Polideportivo Almería* were expelled from division three during the 2000-01 season and then wound up due to financial problems, the *Almería Club de Fútbol* was renamed the *Unión Deportiva Almería* in an attempt to regroup football in the town.

and Zaragoza. 'His style was old school, shall we say. But he saved the club and laid the foundations that Unai could build on. He was also the coach who gave me most belief in myself,' says Ortiz. 'From the very first days when the boss was in charge, it was like a leap forward in time, in technology. We had already used videos now and again, but not like we did with Unai. He paused the images at the exact moment he wanted in order to analyse them, to show for example in what situation our opponent could hurt us, etc. His methodology was an almost abrupt change for me, because I'd never known a trainer working that way before. And I wasn't the only one who thought that.' The first training sessions were innovatory, perhaps too much so for players accustomed to the Spanish second and third divisions.

'Before the sessions, he would get us together to explain the aim of the training and what it would do for us collectively,' explains Laurent de Palmas, a French right-winger who had played for Nîmes, Cannes and Ferrol. 'There was a discussion of tactics, we watched videos, talked. Once he called me out to the front and I had to reply to his questions: "Laurent, you have a throw-in twenty metres out from our goal. What's the first recommended solution? The second? The third? The same for attacking throw-ins. We had to make the most of every detail: how should I position my body to control the ball in such and such a way, to pass it at such and such an angle?"' His rival Bruno Saltor adds: 'He helped me enormously with controlling the ball, especially the ideal position of the body to receive it. And other details, like making the keeper always aim for a player's best foot when taking a goal-kick. He would stop the training if they didn't do that, for example.'The start of the season was approaching, and things were looking good for Almería, whose squad boasted a subtle mix of stability, experienced players and three internationals who ought to bring something extra: the Dutch goalkeeper Sander Westerveld, the Peruvian defender Santiago Acasiete and the Nigerian striker Kalu Uche. 'We were quoted as being among the favourites, but the real favourites were Valladolid. There were lots of clubs pushing for promotion that year: Albacete, Numancia, Cádiz, Tenerife and Málaga,' lists Saltor, who could have added Alavés (finalists in the UEFA Cup against Liverpool in 2001), Gijón and Elche, who regularly yoyoed between *La Liga* and the

Segunda. This long list meant that some supposedly big teams, such as Málaga and Las Palmas, found themselves struggling.

Almería lost the first three matches, against Tenerife (0-1), Real Murcia (2-3) and Salamanca (0-2). 'After our third defeat, I told a journalist that if we didn't change our style of play we would never climb up the table,' Francisco Rodríguez recalls. 'The next day, during training, Unai called me into his office. When I went in I saw the newspaper open on the table, with what I'd said on the front page: "Either we change or we won't succeed." Unai asked me to sit down. "What needs to change is you," he told me. "Either you change your attitude, or you won't be in this team." He was completely correct. And despite the doubts all around him after those three matches because people were questioning his lack of experience, he stayed confident in his own ability.'

One of the other old hands in the dressing room, the midfielder Fernando Soriano, adds: 'We even heard rumours that if we lost the fourth game, he would be sacked. Emery paid no attention and carried on in his usual way: "A football club is like the four legs of a table. One leg is the players, the second the hierarchy, the third the fans, and the fourth the press. If any of these four comes a cropper, the balance is upset. And if three of them fail, it falls over."'

Sunday 17 September 2006. Noon. The *Rojiblancos* (red and whites, the Almería team colours) were at home to another Andalusian team, Cádiz, whose fans are as exuberant as they are eccentric, as shown by one of their favourite chants, often heard late at night in big Spanish cities: 'Drink, drink, drink, drink... we came to get drunk, we couldn't give a damn about the result!' Unfortunately, the Cadiz players obviously weren't in such a festive mood. The match was littered with fouls, like in the good old days of the *furia*. The problem was that refereeing had moved on since then and punished any infractions: the visitors got five yellow cards, and Almería two reds. In spite of this, Emery's men held on to win 2-1 thanks to the dynamic duo of Miguel Ángel Corona (1 metre 75, who first played for Real Madrid, but without success) and Albert Crusat Domènech (1 metre 64, formerly of Espanyol). 'We thought that Kalu Uche was our quickest player, but in fact it was Albert. He shot like a bullet down the left-hand side and didn't care if you passed the ball fifty metres ahead of him,' says Ortiz with a smile.

'I was often on the right, and let's say I had a different style. I liked to have the ball at my feet, to centre it, to win free-kicks or shoot. Thanks to the importance Unai gave to wide players, I had the freedom to come inside and have several possibilities for a pass: up to the striker, out to the wing, or to a midfielder coming to back me up. That meant the defender couldn't cover them all, and I always had options.'

As the weeks went by, Almería found their rhythm, with a big group of players used regularly: 21 players appeared at least 10 times in championship matches, and 17 of them were in the starting line-up more than 10 times. 'Personally, I didn't play a lot (13 games and three goals) but I have great memories of that season and of Unai. That's extraordinary because normally when you're on the bench a lot you're angry with the trainer,' says Francisco, who had scored 36 goals in 103 games for Almería between 2002 and 2004. 'He was very good at dealing with subs. I remember one incident. I hadn't played for five games, and when I got in on that Monday I was annoyed, really upset. But during the training session that morning I had the impression that I'd been playing, because Unai treated me exactly the same as the others. He was watching me so closely that I was sure I would be picked for the following Sunday. But no, I didn't play then either [*laughter*]. He always looked after the substitutes, involving them in everything that was done, giving them a real part to play.'

This feeling is confirmed by Laurent de Palmas, who was often left on the bench in favour of Bruno Saltor. 'I didn't always start a game, but I always felt close to Unai. I knew I was important to the group because of the confidence he gave me. I'm not an easy character, so we had several arguments over the year, but they were always face-to-face, which I appreciated. He's not the kind of trainer who talks behind your back. If he wants to dress you down, he'll do so directly. [...] Towards the end of the season, we were losing 0-2 at half-time to Málaga. In the dressing room Unai made me feel terrible, lower than low. Juan Carlos even told him to calm down, he was going too far. My teammates were gobsmacked, because I hadn't been much worse than others. But I knew why he was on my case. Shortly before, I'd received an offer from Elche, and we'd talked about it. They were offering me a good contract, but Unai asked me to wait until the end of the season to find out if I'd be given another year at Almería. He knew how to talk to everyone, and that day he got at me because he knew I'd react: "You're such a good player, but where are you? Hey, where exactly are you, *joder!*" That got me so mad that in the second half I played a blinder. I think we won 3-2 (in fact, it was a 2-2 draw) and I helped create both goals.'

Psychology, commitment, and a boundless passion for his profession: these qualities confirm what Unai had shown at Lorca, with the added advantage of the presence of Carcedo. 'You can't separate their success,' Saltor agrees. 'Unai could, for example, be tougher on the players because he knew that Juan Carlos was more measured, closer to us.' A closeness obviously helped by the fact that Carcedo was the assistant. 'Unai was the head coach, so he couldn't be as friendly with the players,' Juan Carlos confirms. 'He really likes to talk to his players, he likes to feel there's a bond. He's not a manager who thinks it's enough to observe them from a distance, keeping a strictly professional approach. And yet he's well aware that his prerogatives are different to mine or the other members of the staff. If I see players having a hard time, it's my job to approach them, encourage them and allow them to confide in me more easily than if they had to go and see Unai [...] Honestly, there's nothing extraordinary about it. It can be a change that a player wants, so I give him my advice. We discuss it, and I pass it on to Unai if I think it's necessary. It's the same if a player wants a day off for some reason or other.'

Whereas Carcedo himself is very modest about his role, almost everyone in the club stresses how important it was, especially de Palmas. 'He did a real lot for me. Even after I left the club, we kept in touch. When you're winning, you feel on top of the world, but it wasn't just that. It was the way the pair of them observed, listened, spoke. Unai and Juan Carlos were the pinnacle of the people I met in my career, both in human and in sporting terms.'

Saturday 19 May 2007, 6 p.m. Even though it was early in the evening, Almería was already buzzing, the streets packed, especially in the east of the town. A crowd dressed in red and white converged on the Estadio de los Juegos Mediterráneos, a stadium built for the 2005 Mediterranean Games. In half an hour's time, Almería were due to play Ponferradina, the 38th game of the season in *Segunda*. A rather routine fixture, apparently at least. 'After those first three defeats, we found our rhythm, our style of play. As the season progressed we got better and better, and climbed up the table,' Fernando Soriano recalls gleefully. 'I had a knee injury that left me on the bench for four months. That meant I could spend a lot of time with Unai and see what he was thinking. I could really see his obsession with small details, his wish to control everything. Nothing was left to chance. There was nothing casual about his success.'

The time when some people were wondering if the young Basque trainer should be sacked was in the dim and distant past. 'Honestly, we never had any doubt about Unai. He's obsessed with winning and has the balls to match. He's not very strong, but he's scared of no one. He used to tell us that was his Basque legacy,' laughs de Palmas. The Almería team had the same approach week after week, becoming the only ones able to keep pace with Valladolid thanks to a stunning attack (73 goals by the end of the season, the best in the second division). Conclusion: playing Ponferradina at home with five games to go was synonymous with escape from the division. 'We had been waiting to get back into *La Liga* since 1981. Twenty-six years of abstinence is a long time,' says José Ortiz with a smile. He was in the starting line-up, as usual cheered on to the pitch by a huge crowd of more than 15,000. Unfortunately, as had happened at Lorca six days earlier (where Almería lost 1-3) the start of the game was disappointing, with Ponferradina scoring after seven minutes. Silence. Almería had fluffed its lines, made mistake after mistake. Although Ponferradina were going to be relegated, they dominated the game. What had happened to 'the most seductive team in the division,' in the words of Luis César Sampedro?

Old-timers were already blaming the skies, the heavens that had always been stingy with water – the region around Almería is the driest in Europe, with some spots like Cabo de Gata with annual rainfall of no more than 200mm. Was this yet another curse, as if the people of Almería were destined to be at the mercy of the elements as well as being unable to re-join the top flight of Spanish football?

'One of the things I love about my province,' says Ortiz, 'is that it's full of mystery, stories and legends.' These myths come mainly from the films shot in the desert of Tabernas, about 30 kilometres outside the town. Clint Eastwood, Charles Bronson, Henry Fonda, Sean Connery;

they all earned their spurs there. According to one of the urban myths, they even paid for a round of drinks for all the local extras recruited for the occasion, along with soldiers from Franco's army, to make the films even more realistic. Sergio Leone, the famous Italian director, never left anything to chance, not even the tiny, insignificant details nobody sees. That's what real maestros do, the ones whose sensibility is so developed that they invent, position, cut and recut all the time. 'The whole week, all the effort goes to ensuring that the players are best organised to make it possible to defeat their opponents. I can have an influence, but it will always be limited. I can be positive, stay active, but I'm not out on the pitch,' asserts Unai Emery.

Of course, the manager didn't need to be on the pitch: José Ortiz knew his role to perfection and caught fire at the moment when the prize of a place in *La Liga* seemed to be slipping away. He scored the equalizer. The shots rained in, and Ponferradina buckled. Kalu Uche and Corona finished the job: 3-1, in a perfect remake of *The Good, the Bad, and the Ugly*. Ortiz the good guy, who at the final whistle got hold of a jersey belonging to Juan Rojas, the mythical figure of football in Almería, the man who scored their first ever goal in the *Liga*, in 1979. 'He was my idol. A right-winger who achieved the feat of playing in every division in Spain, from the regional ones to the top division,' José tells me. He himself had just done something similar, climbing from the third division to *La Liga* with his local club. 'I was really young back then, so I don't remember ever having seen him play. But I do remember the articles in the press and the fact that everybody was talking about him the whole time, about everything he had done for Almería. Besides, he was part of the family, because he was my sister's father-in-law. So, to score that day, to score that goal in a game that meant my team was returning to the top division… I couldn't dream of a better day, a finer symbol. Just talking about it again moves me.' With reason: Juan Rojas had died suddenly of a heart attack seven years earlier. All the press and lovers of football spared him a thought that 19 May 2007, wishing he had been there. But they were wrong: he was there, still on the right-wing, warding off the famous curse with one of his brilliant dribbles. Unless that was his successor – a good film never reveals all its mysteries!

Hondarribia in the Basque Country region of Spain, Gipuzkoa – where the heart of the Emery family lies.

(Jon Chica)

Unai back in Hondarribia as guest on cookery programme *No es pais para sosos* with hosts Ander Gonzalez (left) and Ramón Roteta (right).

(EITB)

Unai celebrating after guiding Almeria to their first ever promotion to Spain's top division in 2007.

In charge of Almeria against Real Madrid in September of their debut Primera Division season – where he lead them to an 8th placed finish.

The day Unai was presented as the new head coach of Valencia - 23 May 2008.

(Juan Carlos Cardenas/Epa/Shutterstock)

His arrival in Valencia meant Unai's first season in a European competition that he would later master.

(Srdjan Suki/Epa/Shutterstock)

Unai appointed his former coach in Hondarribia Mikel Jauregi to work alongside him at the Mestalla.

Unai with Juan Mata before Valencia's meeting with Manchester United in the
Champions League in 2010.
(Epa/Shutterstock)

A cold Thursday night in Stoke. Unai in the dug-out at the Brittania Stadium as
Valencia advanced over two legs in the Europa League in 2012.
(Lindsey Parnaby/Epa/Shutterstock)

The next job – Spartak Moscow in 2012.

(Manu Fernandez/Epa/Shutterstock)

The Russian experience would take him back to Spain to face Barcelona. It would be only six months before he returned to the country permanently.

(Manu Fernandez /AP/Shutterstock)

14th elite coaches forum at the Uefa headquarters in Nyon Switzerland in
September 2012 alongside some familiar faces and rivals.
(Salvatore Di Nolfi/Epa/Shutterstock)

Shaking hands with
Sevilla President Jose
Maria Del Nido.
The next chapter begins.
(Raul Caro/Epa/Shutterstock)

Competitive in a different sporting arena.

Preparing his Sevilla team at the start of a Europa League winning streak that would last for three seasons.

8.1

A THROW OF THE DICE

Almería isn't known as the most exuberant town in Andalusia. Of course, people go wild during its festival or the Spring Break in Mojácar, a pretty coastal village in the province, but no more than anywhere else. 'I played for Almería and Málaga. I like Almería a lot, but it's smaller and less lively. In Málaga... there's more excitement, in the bars and in the stadium,' says Emmanuel Dorado, a French defender who was with the two clubs at the start of the 2000s. 'When we won the division two title with Málaga, the city went wild. Thousands of people in the streets, a giant parade, people were completely crazy. We were asked to go out everywhere, and to have meals with everyone.' A Spanish habit lived perhaps even more fervently in Andalusia, where the festive spirit reigns. 'On the day after the game with Ponferradina, I really realised what we had done,' says Ortiz, the team captain. 'At the start of each season we lay a wreath to our patron saint, the Vírgen del Mar, above all to ask for her aid. Whenever we achieve something important, we do the same. But that day, the church was full to overflowing! There were so many people outside we had to make a narrow passage so that we could get in to lay the flowers in honour of our patron. On the day of our promotion, you couldn't walk in the centre of the town because it was so crowded. And the following week it was even worse.'

It wasn't merely a popular event, but also a political one. 'José Ortiz, Unai and myself were awarded medals by the town,' recalls

Francisco Rodríguez, a born-and-bred Almerían. 'But that gold medal doesn't belong just to me, it belongs to all twenty-five of us. But I was given it because I was born here and had played for the club for several years.' A former member of the Espanyol youth team and Valencia reserves, Francisco played for several Almerían teams: Plus Ultra CF, Club Polideportivo Almería and Unión Deportiva Almería, for whom he scored 45 goals. 'Some time after our promotion was confirmed, Unai explained he wasn't counting on me for *La Liga*. That hurt because it was my dream to play in the top division for my home team, the team in my blood. I looked him in the eye and said: "Okay, sack me if you're capable of it". I was the top goalscorer in the club's history, an important man here. And all we players are great egoists. I don't think there's anyone in the world of work who is more egoistical than football players. Even when I said that, Unai was capable of getting rid of me, but in a very elegant way [*laughter*]. He always allowed me to train with the group, never on my own. By doing so, he was showing I wasn't up to being in his team. I realised that from the training sessions, and so I decided to leave [for Granada 74, in the *Segunda*]. He's someone who's very elegant in all the decisions he makes. He'll never hurt a player, it's not in his make-up. His choices are always for the good of the team, and he couldn't give a damn if you're an important guy, a veteran or a young player.' Tough but fair? Francisco agrees: he doesn't bear him any grudge. On the contrary: it was Emery who inspired him to become a trainer. 'He surprised me enormously in every respect. It was thanks to my experience with him that I was attracted to the world of coaching. He influenced my decision to become a trainer after my playing career because I saw in him things I liked and shared [...] He was always certain of his choices. Whenever he announced his starting eleven, he managed to convince the whole dressing room it was the best possible line-up, because he had a certain way of looking at you... His gaze was always frank, transparent. It was obvious he simply wanted the best for the team.'

In the same way, Emery also influenced Laurent de Palmas, who left after only one season with Elche. 'Nowadays I train young players and draw a lot of my inspiration from the work done by Unai and Juan

Carlos. When he becomes a coach, every player takes something from all the coaches he's known. Obviously from Unai I learnt to press, to position my body and to synchronise the whole team.' The same goes for Fernando Soriano, the Zaragoza midfielder, an adopted Almería stalwart.[11] 'He's my role model, honestly. You don't imitate someone, but you take as reference points what was good and avoid what was bad. Thanks to Unai, I learnt the profession while I was still playing. I remember that he always carried a notebook where he wrote down lots of little details. I would read it occasionally, and some of the notes were ten years old, from when he had been a player! He wrote down tactics, the approach to a game, defensive positions, set pieces, everything.'

And more than the purely footballing aspect, these former players who have become coaches recall the way that Unai managed a group and transmitted his message, sometimes in a theatrical way. 'He would dramatize different situations. Once he was talking about the virtues of being a united team and picked up a nearby bucket. He started giving it tremendous kicks. "We'll get rid of it *a patadas* [by kicking it out]! We'll get rid of it, we don't want it with us, we don't want it in the team! He did the same with a plastic bottle, to show the importance of us all being united. In other words, if a player doesn't accept the collective message, we're all going to get rid of him by kicking his arse! Obviously, moments like that make an impression, and helps fix the message in your head.'

***

Sunday 25 August 2007, 6 p.m. The *Rojiblancos* walk across the pitch at the Riazor stadium, the home of Deportivo de La Coruña. In an hour's time, they'll be playing for the first time in *La Liga*, a competition that many of them have only seen on the TV or from the stands as supporters. 'Everyone was saying we had to sign players from the top division, but Unai didn't really agree,' explains the new sporting director, a certain Alberto Benito, a former teammate of

---

11 Arriving in 2005, Soriano stayed with Almería from then on, and in May 2016 became the first-team manager. That season, he succeeded in preventing the club from being relegated to *Segunda B*.

Unai's at Toledo ten years earlier. 'We always stayed friends. When Roberto Olabe left, Unai recommended me to his president, and I came. We worked together and he mentioned two players he most wanted to sign, both of them attacking players from the *Segunda*: Alvaro Negredo and Henok Goitom. We got Negredo, who was playing for the Castilla, Real Madrid's reserve team, but Goitom signed for Murcia.' Juanma Ortiz, a midfielder from Ejido, also joined the squad, along with a few players from the lower divisions who had some experience of the top level (David Cobeño, the second-string goalkeeper at Seville; Pulito, a defender at Getafe, and Juanito, a midfielder from the youth team at Málaga), as well as the historic right-back from Real Sociedad, Aitor López Rekarte. Two Brazilians were also signed: the goalkeeper Diego Alves from Atlético Mineiro and Felipe Melo, a midfielder who came to Spain in 2005 without much success. 'He was a failure at Mallorca, and his experience at Santander wasn't very good either. We knew he hadn't progressed, but that's exactly why we were able to sign him! Previously he was out of reach financially for a club like ours, but now... We knew he had a great footballing talent and it was a risk worth taking. He made an effort, and so did we,' Benito explains.

New recruits or not, Unai Emery wasn't going to leave the players who had won promotion on the bench. But who could tell what he was plotting? Not his captain, for one: 'We had no idea of the starting eleven, not even the goalkeeper. He didn't give us a clue during the preparations for the match,' Ortiz recalls. 'Then it came to the pre-match talk. Unai stared at us for a moment: "I couldn't give a damn who plays. I'm going to throw the dice to decide. I'll write down all your numbers, then throw the dice eleven times. I couldn't give a damn which of you starts because I know you're going to do it. I know we're going to win anyway, whether it's you, you, or you who is on the pitch. I know it." I was annoyed because we all wanted to start, but that talk he gave... it stayed in my memory. It was a demonstration that the team comes before the player, the collective before the individual: I can throw the dice and no matter what comes out, I believe in all of you.'

Ortiz finally came on in the second half, together with Kalu Uche, another player who had helped Almería gain promotion. In the starting eleven, Bruno Saltor, Santiago Acasiete, Mané, Albert Crusat, Corona and Soriano began as they had done the previous season. Not forgetting Juanma Ortiz and Negredo, the two recruits from the *Segunda*. 'Almost nobody had played in *La Liga*, but that didn't matter to Unai. In the end, we won 3-0', continues the record-holder for the number of appearances for the club. A perfect start for the club with the smallest budget in the championship, and soon the ambition was more than to stay up. 'Of course, that was our first aim, because we had been promoted. But I don't think are many promoted teams who go to the Santiago Bernabeu stadium thinking they will win. We talked about it with Unai, and we were sure we could do it,' says Benito.

The players felt the same, among them Albert Crusat, who was in the starting line-up that day in Madrid. 'Barcelona, Real Madrid or Villarreal: Unai never looked for a draw. He only thought about victory and how to get it. He wanted us to go forward, to score goals. It's not the approach you think you'll hear at a club like Almería.' In fact, the team from Andalusia lost 1-3 in the Spanish capital with a goal by Higuain in the 88th minute, but that wasn't the main thing. 'We were respected wherever we went. And we were never thrashed, even at Barça [0-2, with a goal by Messi in the 81st minute]. Our spirit of solidarity prevented that,' continues the winger, a fixture on the left. This solidarity obviously depended a lot on the established players, but also on the way of life instilled by the club's staff.

'We liked to do things together, planning dinners, going out to have a drink, organising a cocktail. Those were very important moments, because they created a link between everyone. The more people are connected, the more they are committed,' confirms Juan Carlos Carcedo. 'Being able to talk about things apart from football creates the conditions for forming a good team. Not all clubs see that as an important consideration for success, but we did. We were also lucky to find people willing to accept our methods. It was an experience… [*he pauses*] A great time. It was a great time. The kind of dressing room I like.'

A dressing room that was buzzing, with José Ortiz acting as a perfect guide for the newcomers to the town. 'José and I liked to help the new boys to feel at home in our town,' Francisco confirms. 'The year we were promoted, we celebrated something almost every week, it was almost an obligation. Unai would tell us every two weeks: "Tonight we're going to have dinner together!"' The staff took part in even the most festive events. 'The Christmas meal the previous year was something else,' laughs Ortiz. 'An evening with lots of drink when we played Secret Santa. A few days earlier, each of us had drawn the name of the person we had to give a present to. At Christmas you get the present, but you don't know who gave it to you. Some of the presents were… [*he bursts out laughing*]. We had such a good time. It was an evening none of us would forget, Unai included. It's the sign of a team that lives together.'

Despite winning promotion and having the cameras trained on the *Rojiblancos*, the atmosphere in the team was always relaxed. 'Because of Unai there was a lot of press coverage. The press was interested in him because of his age and his trajectory. Also, because he was always pacing up and down on the touchline, he was often on TV. And it was lucky that the cameras didn't follow us on board the bus after the games. When he relaxes and starts to drink, it's quite extraordinary,' laughs Crusat.

These shared moments concealed a huge amount of work. Following Emery's arrival in Andalusia, his players gave him a nickname: the *'enfermo de fútbol'*. 'We called him that because he really is ill with football. He drinks football, eats football, sleeps football, and we wondered whether he didn't fuck football,' smiles de Palmas. This view is confirmed by Fernando Soriano, the conveyor belt of the Almería midfield. 'I've known all kinds of trainers. Unai was by far the most perfectionist and the hardest worker. By far. That was all he thought about.' The only concern was his volcanic temperament, sometimes not always measured in the substitutions he made. 'I'll remember a game against Betis all my life,' says Bruno Saltor, in the starting line-up 34 times that season. 'Negredo opened the scoring, but then we picked up two red cards in the first half-hour [the defender Santiago Acasiete in the 14th minute and the goalkeeper

David Cobeño in the 23rd]. We gave away a penalty and were losing 1-2. There must have been twenty minutes left, and Unai took off a midfielder and brought on an attacker [Crusat for Natalio]. I couldn't believe it, because there were only nine of us. But Unai couldn't have cared less, he wanted to win, and too bad if they scored another goal – which they did, and we lost 1-3.'

That defeat, on 16 December, was a turning point in Almería's season. The suspension of the goalkeeper Cobeño gave an opportunity to Diego Alves, who had already shone in the victory against Seville (1-0). The Brazilian shored up an occasionally hesitant defence as well as the rest of the team. 'We were a bit uneven; the players needed time to meet the demands of this top level. Some of the players pulled the team upwards, like the newly arrived Brazilian midfielder Felipe Melo, who had spent the first four games on the bench,' says Benito. 'Unai knew Melo was intrinsically better than the others, but he arrived at the very end of the transfer market with a very poor reputation after his previous experience in Spain. First of all, he had to win the respect of the dressing room, and Unai had told him that clearly.' Although he had a tendency to explode (13 yellow cards in 34 matches) and 'gave the impression of being capable of killing someone on the pitch at any moment' according to his teammates, he was an essential part of a devastating start to the new year that saw Almería unbeaten in seven games: five wins and two draws. The high point was the game against Real Madrid on 2 February. 'I was rooming with Carlos Garcia, and our room overlooked the pitch. The president of Real [Ramón Calderón] arrived and gave a speech to all the Madrid *peñas*', says Ortiz. 'It was full of people from Almería. When the interview began, a fan shouted: "*Vamos presidente!* We've got to hammer Almería, score lots of goals!" And he was an *Almeriense*, not a *Madrileño*. We watched it all from our window and said to ourselves: "What? Did you hear that?" We left our room in a real stink. We mentioned it to the others in the dressing room, and Unai took advantage of it. Real Madrid was unbeaten in 10 or 12 games [nine wins and one draw] and they weren't worried about coming here. Their president talked as if they were all that was best in football, and I don't know what else. Unai took advantage of this to motivate us. When he had finished, we ran out onto the pitch like madmen to show Madrid they weren't invincible.' The result: Almería 2-Real Madrid 0.

Almería's second half of the season won praise all round. Barcelona also came a cropper at the Estadio de los Juegos Mediterráneos (2-2), while the *Rojiblancos* thrashed Seville away (4-1). 'That was probably the finest match of my whole career,' Soriano says proudly. The club not only stayed up, they almost qualified for the now defunct Intertoto Cup. Unfortunately, as with Mallorca (who finished in seventh place), Almería did not register in time, and the slot went to La Coruña (in ninth place). Even so, with 52 points from 38 games, Unión Deportiva Almería finished eighth, the club's highest position ever. Unai Emery was equal fourth for the Trofeo Miguel Muñoz, awarded to the best manager in *La Liga*, only three points behind the winner, Manuel Pellegrini, then manager of Villarreal.

'Years later, people still talk to me of the Emery years,' Ortiz says. 'In every interview, I get asked how I felt when we won promotion. I often respond: "And how did you feel as a supporter?" "It was incredible, the best thing I've ever known!" "Then just think how I felt deep down inside when I played and scored in the game that won us promotion, and then wore my home team's jersey in *La Liga*! I was just like you, another fan out there on the pitch." I've never known anything so great apart from the birth of my two children. Almería had never had such a squad and such success, and that was thanks to Unai.

'No Almería supporter can forget that, above all me! I send him a message each anniversary because of all we lived through… [*he pauses*]. At the time, we knew he wasn't going to stay long. We talked about it among us. The president tried to keep him, and we thought for a while it would be possible, although we knew it wasn't. He was destined for something more.'

8.2

INTERVIEW WITH ALVARO NEGREDO

Starting his career at Rayo Vallecano, the club of his Madrid neighbourhood (Vallecas), Alvaro Negredo went on to join the Real Madrid reserves at Castilla, then in the *Segunda*. Overshadowed by Roberto Soldado in his first season, he scored 18 goals in the next. In spite of requests from more glamorous clubs, he decided to sign for Almería when only 22. His success there (13 and then 19 goals in two seasons) led him on to Seville, Manchester City, Valencia and the Spanish national side, with whom he won the European Championships in 2012.

Arrival at Almería

'I had several offers, but I came here after a talk with Unai. What he said, the way he talked to me, the fact that he made me feel his joy and enthusiasm at having me for this dream of being in *La Liga*... I thought about that a lot and came here. I was lucky enough to start in *La Liga* and to find a positive dressing room. We knew we were a club of modest means, but with the bonding there was, all that going out together, those dinners, really created a sense of dynamism. No one expected us to finish so high up the table, and I think that human side helped a lot.'

What Emery expects of an attacking player

'Given my build and height [1.86 metres and more than 85 kilos], there's no doubt my physique doesn't allow me always to press or to fetch the ball from deep. The main idea was to push up against the defence so that our midfield could intercept the ball as high up the pitch as possible and then pass it to the player up front, who was meant to distribute it at once to the wide players. I had to be part of a team effort, even if people often said that the team was playing for me [*laughter*]. The most important thing was the way Unai trusted me. I learnt a lot of things from him: sustained effort individually and collectively, perseverance. But above all it was a matter of trust. I remember a game against Valladolid that we won 1-0. We had a free-kick about twenty-five metres from goal. Corona passed the ball to me, I hit it on the volley and it flew into the net! We had practised the routine at least fifteen times in training that week: I didn't score once [*laughter*]. Before the game, Unai came up to me and said: "If you can, give it a go!" Then when we won a free-kick in a similar position, I told a teammate we should try it. Another guy said: "You're crazy, you missed them all in training! We're not going to do it!" I told him I was confident, and he let me try. Corona laid the ball on for me and I hit it like never before. It was a crazy idea, because we didn't normally play free-kicks like that, but Unai liked to take risks.'

The team-talks

'Unai surprised me a lot, because none of his team-talks were the same. Each match was a different one. I remember one pre-match session when we were in the hotel in a room watching a video of the opposing team. The images flashed by, but Unai didn't say a word. He was watching us closely but didn't speak. And so, of course, we looked back at him, wondering when he was going to start talking. All of a sudden, he stared straight at me, so I stared back at him as hard as I could. He moved on to another teammate, who had the same reaction. Then another one, who asked Unai: "What's going on?" He wasn't trying to confront him, he simply asked the question because he was wondering why Unai wasn't talking, as he usually did. This went on for a long while! Then Unai told him straight out: "Alvaro is concentrating, he's already thinking what he has to do. So is he – he's trying to read the opposition's defence. But you're not focusing on the game." The next day, coincidence or not, that player was sent off. Those few words have stayed in my mind because simply by looking at us, he knew what people were thinking. And by chance, our teammate got a red card the following day that cost us the match…'

Who is Unai Emery?

'An "enfermo de fútbol" [*laughter*]. I think he lives and breathes football twenty-four hours a day. The way he lives it, puts it into practice, brings it into everyday life, creates a sense of passion in all his players. Personally, he succeeded in bringing out the best in me. I think he developed things I never even imagined were there. He knows how to stress the human side with his psychological approach, and he gives you the confidence, the freedom for everyone to express themselves on the pitch. I've known coaches who force you to play in such and such a way, who stop you trying certain things. Unai never did that. In training, he was always sure that we would do things well. He had more confidence in his players than we had in ourselves.'

9

THE LEGEND OF ELDORADO

Juan Sánchez is a man of few words on first meeting. 'I don't like to boast,' he confesses shyly after meeting his daughter from school. Yet he was the one responsible for bringing Emery to Valencia despite the challenges of appointing such a young manager (Unai was 36 at the time). 'There was a lot of talk of Emery in Spain. His rise impressed everyone, and he was soon going to be out of contract,' explains Alberto Benito, the sporting director at Almería. 'I called my friend Juan, who was technical director at Valencia. I knew that whatever we did, we couldn't keep Unai, so I recommended him to Valencia.'

Emery and Sánchez agreed on a preliminary meeting that required the utmost discretion because of the competition. They quickly agreed on where to meet: in Lorca. 'The meeting took hours. We started talking football and he couldn't stop. He explained what he thought of our season, our players, what we needed to work on. When I got back to Valencia I was delighted: I knew he was our man. He's someone with enormous belief in himself and his abilities. And during our discussion, he had managed to convey that confidence, that self-assurance, to me. Then all Sánchez had to do was convince all the leading figures in the club. 'The other people wanted a better-known name, someone with more experience. Emery was still a novice manager and was bound to make mistakes, but it was a bet we had to take.' At the end of May 2008 Emery signed a two-year contract with the *Murciélagos*, who had finished a poor tenth in the *Liga* the previous season, with a goal difference of minus 14. 'The idea was finally to bring some stability. That was my plan, and Unai fitted it perfectly. He had the advantage of achieving a lot with scarce resources. And at that moment, Valencia wasn't in a very good situation,' admits Sánchez, referring to the construction of the club's new stadium, Nou Mestalla. This grandiose project had begun a year and a half earlier, and was expected hold 75,000 fans. 'All over the city, and in the province as a whole, that was a period of a crazy real estate boom,' according to François Miguel Boudet, a Franco-Spanish journalist based in the Valencia region. 'We were living in a kind of bubble. Buildings were springing up everywhere, with no thought of tomorrow.'

At the start of the new millennium, Valencia seemed not to have a care in the world. There were plenty of jobs, mass tourism on its coast, and the city bars celebrated the success of its football team, top of the *Liga* in 2002 and 2004, winners of the UEFA Cup against Marseilles in 2004, and of the European Supercup against Porto, also in 2004. So, *joder*, why worry? Cañizares, Ayala, Rufete, Vicente, Mista or Miguel Ángel Angulo provided plenty of reasons to smile at life, what did it matter that Rafael Benitez had left for Liverpool?

'The problem was that we had never succeeded in finding a good fit after he had gone. The managers came and went, but it didn't work, because they weren't given enough time,' says Sánchez. The problem was the Mestalla, which quickly exhausted managers. 'The fans are... make no mistake, I loved playing here,' says Juan Mata. 'It's a great club, a very great one even. But there's so much passion that when things go badly it has terrible repercussions in the city. And it's true that managers don't always have an easy life here, quite the opposite in fact,' he says with a little laugh. Starting out at Oviedo and then playing for Real Madrid reserves, he was only 20 when Emery joined the '*ches*'. 'I had only been playing for one season, and it had been a difficult one. The manager [Ronald Koeman] had been sacked, and we ended up with our press spokesman as coach.[12] We still managed to win the Copa del Rey, but the club needed a fresh start.'Following Benitez, no manager had lasted more than two seasons: Ranieri, López Habas, Quique Sánchez Flores, Koeman and Voro took turns in the dugout, all without success. 'I'm from here, I've played here and worked here. I think I know what the place is like, Juan Sánchez continues. 'Valencia is the toughest club, the one that demands the most of its players. The people here sometimes forget we're not Barça or Real Madrid. We don't have the same resources, even if we have incredible supporters and a great city behind us. We were able to compete and win at one point, but then the financial crisis made it impossible. Impossible.'

The famous crisis that no one saw coming – especially not the property developers and politicians such as Mariano Rajoy, until 2018 the prime minister of Spain, who used to quote Valencia as the model of a fine future – arrived soon after Emery had signed for Valencia. It was a sign, but a sign of what? Of the ability to throw away 150 million euros, as was the case with the still barely used airport of Castellón-Costa Azahar, 100 kilometres north of the city? Opened in 2011, the airport had to wait until 14 January 2015 to see the first plane take off! And even then, it was a charter flight for the Villarreal club, one of the sponsors of the airport construction, who were playing away to Real Sociedad…In only a few months, Valencia nosedived, like most of Spain. The ambitious building projects turned out to be financial black holes. Just like the former club shirt sponsor at the start of the 2000s: Terra Mítica. Based in Benidorm, the most concreted-over resort in the province of Valencia and probably the whole of Spain, this amusement park cost more than 377 million euros. Terra Mitica promised to recreate 'atmospheres inspired by the pharaohs, ancient Greece or the Roman Empire,' to a backdrop of roller coasters and a nearby motorway. It was a concept about as bright as the fireworks that were let off across the city for a quarter of an hour every evening. 'They didn't know what to do

---

12 Salvador González Marco, known as *Voro*, who took over temporarily several times after Unai had moved on.

with their money,' recalls Mariano, the owner of the Mario Stamcafé
in Benidorm, a bar specialising in Belgian beers. 'So at first they had
brightly coloured rockets that were really spectacular. Then it became
more modest, and only lasted a few minutes. Later it was only the
weekends, and now it's only on holidays.'

The football club met a similar fate: extremely happy to show
off its good fortune at the start of the 2000s, but then: 'Over the
past six years, Valencia spent 300 million more euros than it took in,'
according to the daily *El País* on 8 June 2009. The club's accounts
are blood-curdling, showing a total debt of 547 million euros! Worse
still, the dream of a new stadium evaporated when all building work
stopped in February 2006, because of unpaid contractors.[13]

In the midst of all this, Emery did what he could, as best he
could. 'The club had been rather neglected. Salaries were not being
paid, nobody was taking decisions. For months the situation was
very difficult,' recall Emery's brother Igor. 'There was a crisis of
results [three defeats and three draws in February and March against
opponents from the bottom half of the table]. The only reason Unai
wasn't sacked like the other managers before him was because there
was no real organisation in the club. Nobody had the faintest idea
what was going on.'

In the end, Valencia finished sixth, qualifying for the Europa
League: Unai managed to limit the damage. 'When we came to
Valencia, we had to re-awaken the joy, the passion, in a squad where
a lot of players had won trophies and were resting on their laurels.
Maybe that was what was most important, to rekindle their flame,
their love of football,' says Unai himself. In the meantime, he had lost
Juan Sánchez. his sporting director, who had left after a few months.
'There was so much uncertainty at the club,' Juan Carlos Carcedo
recalls. 'The atmosphere was very different to Almería. It was more
professional, the team was much bigger, and the atmosphere was
terrific for home games against Barça or Real Madrid. But we lived

---

13 It would take another book to detail the club's financial history. In short, the
management had planned to sell off building plots at Mestalla to partially finance the
building of the new stadium, but that never happened.

through things… [*he pauses*] Whenever people talk to me about Valencia, I see the great moments we had, but also all the rest, the natural demands that existed before and after Unai. We hadn't had to deal with that before and wouldn't do so again. It's at that kind of critical moment, when you find yourself all alone in adversity, that everything seems against you… ' Carcedo won't say anything more. His thoughts remain a secret, but Valencia has its effect on everyone, no one more so than a manager and his assistant abandoned to the Mestalla and its swirling winds.

10.1

AFRAID OF NO ONE

In June 2009, Valencia finally announced its recovery plan. This included an increase in the club's capital, a reduction in the wage bill (from 112 million euros a year to 92 million, in the knowledge that the club produced an income of that amount), plus other economies designed to avoid having to sell its best players immediately, apart that is from Raúl Albiol, transferred to Real Madrid for 15 million euros. This new austerity was essential for the survival of the *Murciélagos* and aimed to reduce the total debt to 237 million euros in the space of three years. Ironically, the president appointed to carry this programme out was Manuel Llorente, the general manager from the start of the millennium, that famous epoch when money had flown out of the club...

Having left in December 2005 after disagreements with Juan Soler, a former president and the club's main shareholder, Llorente stepped in again to avoid imminent bankruptcy. 'To do that, we needed above all to qualify for the Champions League. The club's future depended on it, and Unai was well aware of that [...] At our first meeting after my appointment, we met with the sporting director. We sat down and Unai analysed the squad player by player. I've known Valdano, Benitez and lots of other great managers, but that was the first time that I came across such a detailed, meticulous approach.'

That was a first victory for the Basque coach, but the atmosphere was still gloomy, especially after Valencia came only sixth in his first season. 'I kept in touch with Juan Carlos and we talked a lot to one another. The players had their doubts, because some of them no longer really wanted to strive to improve,' says Laurent de Palmas. Unai simply adds: 'I knew very well that some players didn't support the project or the club. But I wasn't going to change my way of doing things for guys like that.'

He was proved right: Valencia finished third in 2010, 2011 and 2012. But the French player's comments touch on one of the limits of Emery's management style: the commitment to a passionate, demanding method. 'He has such a high level of demands on himself that anyone alongside him has no choice but to try to reach the same level,' in the view of Roberto Olabe, the sporting director from Unai's first season at Almería. 'His demands aren't so much physical or technical. They're based on how you can improve, on understanding why things happen. He's terribly demanding about matters like that. So, if you're not willing to commit yourself completely every day, you won't be able to work with him. It'll never succeed.'

The central defender David Navarro puts it even more simply: 'If you're willing to work, you'll explode. If not...' Returning to Valencia in 2009, he had to adapt to the expectations of a manager who demanded he added fresh skills to his legendary toughness. 'He wanted us to take part more in the game, to bring the ball out from the back if possible. And seeing that I was never the most skilled with my feet... [*laughter*] I made a lot of progress in that, in relaunching the attack. In order to do that, I had to reach a level of concentration I'd never had before in that area.'

The effort Unai demanded was not only on the mental level, but on the emotional one as well. 'I think that what would make Unai really sad would be to find himself with a group of players who no longer feel anything for football,' says Albert Crusat, another former Almería player.

Not a smile during training, or the desire to improve, to question oneself, or to leave behind your comfort zone? Take care, because Emery can see red, in the literal sense of the term. 'I'll remember one incident all my life. He pursued a player in the middle of training. He ran after him, tugging on his shirt,' says Adil Rami, who arrived for the last of Unai's four seasons at Valencia. 'Sometimes I see myself in him, because he can be impulsive and he has such a desire to win that sometimes he goes too far. After a game, you can't talk to him! He's already immersed in his match, his replay, it's incredible! But you can say what you like, his way of managing a group shows he's a gentleman. A real gentleman.' A tough but honest method, as his brother Igor explains. 'We're very het-up people. The Emerys are very stubborn, very hard-working and very honest. Which means we're very Basque [*laughter*]. Sometimes we can go too far, but there's always a reason behind what Unai does. He once told me he'd given a player a really hard time during a training session. The player was getting lots of yellow and red cards, and Unai wanted to put him to the test during training. So, he insulted and provoked him without him realising it, in order to teach him self-control. Yeah, that's why training sessions are private: a lot of things that go on there could be taken out of context!'

These misinterpretations were even more frequent at Valencia, where for the first time Emery encountered media pressure that went beyond the local level. 'In the press box at the Mestalla there are at least fifty journalists for every game. They scrutinise and spy on everything. There's an enormous demand locally and that obviously affects the national coverage of the club,' François Miguel Boudet confirms. 'At the start, Emery benefitted from a real appreciation of what he was saying, his ambition. He brought a breath of fresh air, and above all a passion that had been lost.'

His enthusiasm, the images he used to describe things, the way he mimicked people made these observers smile, feel sympathetic towards him. 'You have to choose good rowers, then row, row, row [...] And if anyone doesn't row, he gets thrown overboard,' he would say, matching his words with gestures that the press found hilarious. 'But the atmosphere soon changed,' recalls his brother Igor. 'It became more hostile. Towards the end, it even grew rather hot with some journalists. Concerned with what he wanted to say, Emery didn't hesitate to frown and take journalists to task, especially when they insisted on asking about Valencia's third place in *La Liga,* as the club had done in the three seasons under him. 'Where does that question come from? You have a responsibility for the question you ask a manager! That's basic [...] The whole season we've been playing on Wednesdays and Sundays. That's great for you, because it gives you more news, you sell more papers, but for those of us inside the club it means we get worn down with all the hard work we have to put in, because you have to give a hundred per cent, but that's not always possible. [...] I'm not going to give any negative message, and I don't share your point of view. The second half of the season wasn't so good, and the reason for that was that we didn't stop playing for four months and I couldn't count on some players, others couldn't sustain that rhythm and others didn't manage to play at the same level as in the first half of the season. Coming third is the limit of what we can achieve. And I'm going to celebrate that third place. I'm going to celebrate it! And I'm inviting everyone to do the same, and to enjoy the moment!' Unai exclaimed in May 2012, during his last year at Valencia, when the club finished below Real Madrid and Barça but above all the other challengers for a place in the Champions League: Málaga, Atlético Madrid, Seville and Bilbao.

'I extended Unai's contract, but always one year at a time,' explains the club president, Manuel Llorente. 'We never increased his salary because we didn't have the money. Once we even lowered it. Over the three years, there were always some doubts, particularly in the last one. He said to me with his usual self-confidence: "Manolo, I promise to take the team to third place this season. I promise."

It was a promise that was kept, even though the squad lost its best players and promising youngsters every year. In 2010, David Villa joined Barcelona for 40 million euros and David Silva signed for Manchester City for 33 million. In 2011, Juan Mata was transferred to Chelsea for 28 million euros, while two players from Andalusia, Joaquín and Isco, joined Málaga for more than 10 million. Under Emery, Valencia brought in more than 140 million euros from the sale of players, not counting the transfer of Jordi Alba to Barcelona for 14 million euros the following summer, a player transformed by Emery and his staff.

Mikel Jauregi, Unai's coach when he was an adolescent with Hondarribia and who rejoined him at Valencia, remembers this remarkable transformation. 'Alba was a left-winger in the reserves. He found it hard to win a place there in the first-team, so Unai decided to use him as a wing-back to make better use of his speed. Maybe he wasn't too good at getting past an opponent, but if he ran onto the ball in empty spaces, he gave us more options. At first, Unai played him in that position for a few minutes, sometimes half an hour. Later on, it would be a whole half and, in the end, he was pushing Jérémy Mathieu for his place. For a while, Jordi wasn't convinced, he kept saying he wanted to play in midfield, not out wide. We convinced him by showing him videos and by being very demanding with him, because just as he was very good going forward, he needed not to forget to come back and work in defence. The funny thing about this story is that Jordi was convinced he could have a great career as a winger, but Unai and Carcedo kept telling him he would never be a great winger but could be a great wing back. Jordi is stubborn, but he came up against someone more stubborn than him: Unai *[laughter]*.'

This episode illustrates the hard work Unai had to do to find solutions due to the chronic exodus of players during his last three seasons at the Mestalla. 'He never complained, he never said anything negative to me about selling players, even if it meant we were losing our best ones,' says Llorente, who managed the great achievement of putting the club on a stable footing. 'Nor did he demand that we sign any particular player. Well, it's true he insisted for a long while that we buy Griezmann…'

Unai remembers that story well: 'It was after Mata had left. Griezmann was playing in the *Segunda* with Real Sociedad [39 games, 8 goals] and I knew him very well. A friend of mine, Roberto Olabe, had brought him to our training centre when he was very young. So, I was able to see how he was progressing: we had often talked about it. Unfortunately, not everyone at Valencia shared my opinion.'

This apparently anecdotal episode was symptomatic of Unai's years at Valencia. A sense that his decisions and changes were not really understood. In the game against Leverkusen in the Champions

League on 1 November 2011, the substitution of Pablo Piatti by Feghouli created howls of protest, and a chant aimed directly at Unai: '*Burro, burro, burro!*' Unmoved, the Basque 'donkey' remained out in the technical area at the side of the pitch, absorbing the crowd's anger. 'It was his way of taking the pressure on himself and sparing the substitute and the other players,' says his brother Igor. It was an exchange that ended with Valencia emerging triumphant, winning 3-1.

Another disputed area was the starting line-up, which changed from game to game. 'I used to go and see him at the *Ciudad Deportiva* [training ground] three or four times a week and would ask him why he was doing this or that. Once during a meal, he was studying all the teams he had put out, and all the changes he had made,' says Llorente. I asked him: "How can you change five, six, or even seven players from one line-up to the next?" "No, it's not like that. I change three or four players, at most five." "Look, on average it's five players you change from one game to the next." I said that to him because managers study the game, but not necessarily the statistics. "Oh, so now you're checking up on me, are you? Look, it's all written down here!" He was annoyed, but we both saw the funny side. He would always explain to me why he did things, it was a fascinating dialogue.'

Including all competitions, Emery put out a different eleven in 80 consecutive games! A record that made tongues wag, as did Valencia's elimination in the early stages of the different cup competitions. 'That was the problem in those years. We played great football, we did well in the *Liga,* but we failed in the cup competitions. That's what people most held against the boss,' says Navarro. They lost 2-4 on aggregate to Schalke in the Champions League Round of 16 in 2011, they finished in third place behind Leverkusen in the group stage of the same competition in 2012 and were eliminated in the semi-final of the Europa League (2-5 on aggregate) that same year.

All of this suggested the end of a cycle was near. 'And yet I don't think the fans have a bad memory of the style of play Unai preferred. Especially now, when Valencia has been through several complicated seasons, the job Unai did is appreciated,' adds Juan Sánchez, the former technical director. If Emery is hated at the Mestalla these days, it's absolutely not for his sporting record, but because he went on to Seville, and because of his wild celebrations when they beat Valencia in the semi-finals of the Europa League.' And François Miguel simply adds: 'Let's just say he should have shown more restraint, given the affection he said he had for Valencia.' A pious wish: nobody has ever been able to control Unai on the touchline, not even the fourth official or a crowd baying for him to get lost. 'No one will ever change him,' Alberto Benito confirms. 'I've seen him evolve and seen him fight to keep his job in very difficult situations. As his friend, I've suffered with him, and almost wished he would get fired so that he could be less stressed, but he always wanted to fight, to resist. He didn't have that strength at the beginning. It's the result of a lot of work on his own make-up. When he was a player, he couldn't take pressure. But now he'll fight to the death to achieve his objectives.'

This desire and ambition was just as evident in every match against the two giants of Spanish football, according to his players, like Adil Rami. 'When I was with Lille, I played in the Europa League against Lisbon, Porto and so on: in France, you knew you were going to get a hiding. When I came to Valencia, my first big match was against Barça. So, I was up against Lionel Messi, which is a different world to Porto. Unai gave his pre-match talk: "We're going to play with two wide men out on the left, but not in defence. We're doing it to make life hard for them on their right!" He wanted us to get forward, and if it wasn't one of us, it was the other. Alba and Mathieu destroyed their right-hand side, and we got a draw [2-2]. As we left the field I was proud of myself, and I realised that our coach was one of the big boys. He was afraid of no one.'

By now, Emery had forgotten his fears and doubts. He even posed proudly in March 2012 with his book *Mentalidad Ganadora, el Método Emery*, a psychological and group management essay written in collaboration with Juan Carlos Cubeiro, a teacher and well-known author in the field of leadership and coaching. The book was fairly well received, even if the title was questioned by the Valencia supporters, given the club's poor start in the first part of the 2012 season: knocked out of the Copa del Rey in a semi-final against Barcelona, and only two unimpressive wins in nine games in *La Liga*.

As for the media, they picked up on a passage in the book about Isco: 'He's a talented player with a tendency to be overweight and not always to perform. I've tried to work strategically with Isco, evaluating and analysing every moment of his performance in training and in matches: his commitment, his passes, so that in 2011-12 he could be in the squad and demonstrate his talent at the highest level.'

Isco, who appeared only seven times for Valencia and was sold to Málaga in the summer of 2011, has often reproached Emery for his lack of time on the field. 'Everyone thinks Unai wanted to get rid of him, but he heard about the transfer when he was on holiday and went mad. He wanted to keep Isco, but he couldn't promise him he would start, or how long he would be on the pitch in a match. He never does that for anybody,' says Unai's brother. Something even more difficult at Valencia, where a host of players sat gathering dust in the stands: the Serbia giant Nikola Zigic, the Venezuelan striker Miku, the Italo-Argentine Chori Domínguez, the Nigerian Sunny or the Uruguayan Nacho Gonzalez, who didn't play a single game but was constantly out on loan thanks to his agents doing deals with all the least appetising clubs in the world…

'We had at least thirty players, which made it more difficult for the staff. Unai surprised me, because he succeeded in always making the sessions varied and interesting for everyone. It was always a pleasure to go to training,' David Navarro insists. 'I like that kind of trainer who's passionate, demanding. He always kept whistling to stop play, redo it, correct things. If I had to keep just one image of the boss it would be that: the man with the whistle. Ah no, there was also the whiteboard. That was the first time in my life that I saw a trainer pick up a whiteboard and bring it onto the training pitch.'

Juan Mata laughs out loud when he recalls this: 'It was incredible, because he carried the board out into the middle of the pitch. Then he used his whistle to stop the exercises, start them again, stop, then off again until we reached near-perfection. If I learnt one thing from Unai, it's to stop thinking that details are a matter of chance.'

Details, one of Unai's obsessions during his years with Valencia, like that crazy whiteboard which, according to rumours in the dressing room, was haunted. 'He used it to give quite a few players a nightmare,' laughs Bruno Saltor, who like Unai arrived in 2009 and left in 2012. 'He would ask us questions, and for some of us it was torture trying to explain different systems or even just to answer him [...] Unai liked to use a laser pointer to get us to look when he was teaching something on the whiteboard. Before one of his talks, a player had taken the pointer and hidden it. Unai came into the dressing room and asked where it was because he was going to start his talk. Nobody said a word. When he turned around, the player who had it flashed the beam onto the board. Unai whipped round to try to see who it was. In the end, ten minutes went by, because he couldn't discover the player, and every time he explained something on the board, the laser dot appeared. That was a great moment, because the boss could take a joke.'

This may no longer have been the dressing rooms of Lorca or Almería, but Emery had not changed much. 'His pre-match talks were still just as long, occasionally too long. He liked to analyse life in general and often reflected on topics that weren't necessarily anything to do with football. Some people liked that, others didn't [...] Unai insisted a lot that the path leading to success was more important than the victory itself. At Almería we were a modest team, so we happily accepted all the hard work, especially over tactics. But here, with so many players with great technical ability, it was harder for them to make the effort to understand his tactical approach, the right-back concludes. A reference to the many yawns in evidence during the video sessions, which some found interminable. 'I spent three years with Emery, but I couldn't stand a fourth. He played so many videos I was running out of popcorn...' Joaquin Sanchez laughed as he said this in an interview on *El Partido de las 12* on the Cope radio station. He is also often credited with a repeated declaration that overshadowed his other quote: 'Emery is a man sick with football. He's one of the best managers I ever had, but you have to be able to put up with him.'

It's all a question of personality: no one can be friends with the whole world. 'I'm going to say something important, and I'll go on saying it until people understand. There's nothing nasty about Unai [...] When Unai is working, it's his heart that's talking,' insists Manuel

Llorente. 'I felt that the players saw him as a deeply honest person. He was natural with them, and that's his strong point, his ability to convey a message. He dedicated himself body and soul to his work, and the players, of course, respected that as well. The problem was he was late for every meeting, we always began half an hour late! And he often forgot to eat. I used to have to tell him to have something, because he was skinny enough already!'

Fortunately, Emery used to go to refuel in the evening at Kailuze, a Basque restaurant he ended up owning. In his bad moments, after a defeat when 'what I most want is to hide and disappear for three days, for nobody to see me, for them to forget me,'[14] only the dishes prepared by the chef Elena Saldaña could take him out of himself. Sitting down to *kokotxas de merluza* (hake cooked slowly with garlic, parsley and olive oil) or *bacalao al pil-pil* (cod seasoned with pepper, garlic and olive oil) he travelled back to the Basque country, at least for as long as the dinner lasted, and came back full of energy for the liqueur, the delicious *Izarra* that has left more than a few people under the table. 'I feel like sleeping three days on the trot,' he said after the thrashing by Real Madrid. 'Don't worry, pour me another one, Elena, no one will notice.'

---

14 A declaration Unai made in a press conference following the 3-6 defeat at home to Real Madrid on 23 April 2011.

10.2

INTERVIEW WITH JUAN MATA

Before signing for Valencia in 2007, Juan Mata was the second highest goalscorer for the Real Madrid reserve team, behind Alvaro Negredo. Brought into the squad for his first season as a professional (25 games, 5 goals), he really took off under Emery. Over the next three years, he played 139 matches and scored 37 goals, before going abroad and becoming world champion in 2010.

First impressions

'Every player has different needs. When Unai arrived, I needed to feel really confident, because a player always has doubts. I'd just finished my first year as a professional when we won the Copa del Rey, but I knew deep inside that to consolidate during a second season would be much more difficult. You see a lot of players with huge promise as youngsters, but not many of them succeed in maintaining the same high level. From the first time I met him, I liked the way Unai talked to us. I could feel his confidence and that allowed me to believe more in myself and to grow as a professional. He provided the support I needed at the start of my career.'

The way he was used

'I played as a left midfielder, a number 10 and even wide on the right. I remember a game against Numancia where he put me as striker because the specialists in that position weren't available. That's the only time I've ever played as centre-forward. [*laughter*]. We worked hard on tactics, even the creative and attacking players: what to do when you lose the ball, how to position yourself at specific moments of the game to have a more compact team, etc. Personally, I remember above all the care he took over free-kicks. It was crazy how many different routines we had. We didn't have enough fingers to signal which one it would be [*laughter*]. Unai is the manager who works hardest at strategies for set pieces: corners, free-kicks and throw-ins. And he would change tactics depending on who we were facing. Along with Juan Carlos, he was constantly coming up with new ideas and we won thanks to that several times. We were often surprised, because it could seem very complicated and you had to concentrate a lot, apart from anything else trying to remember what the plan was for different games, because it changed all the time [*laughter*]. Sometimes we would screen a player, at others a short pass, then have another player hit it. I remember above all a free-kick we always used to do in the middle of our opponents' half. Instead of sending the ball up the middle of the pitch where everyone was crowding in, we would put two players on each side and two in the centre. At the sides, one player screened the other, who darted forward towards the far post. The player taking the free-kick would raise an arm to show which side the ball would go. I don't know if Unai still does it, but if it's the right arm, then it's going to the right-hand side [*laughter*].'

The importance of psychology

'The managers I've known all had their own specific way of working. Apart from the set pieces, I think what's special about Unai is the way he communicates. In his talks, he used to write, three, four or five things on the board: those were the points he was going to bring up. Sometimes it was five phrases or metaphors he was going to explain. I've never seen that with my other managers. They usually revolved around phrases about positivity, camaraderie, the values he wanted to create in his team. To do that, he did something no one else did, that is, he communicated by means of the points he had written down. His talks could go on and on because he didn't notice the time and carried on talking, but what he said was always intense, and he would ask you questions. That turned it into a kind of seminar that brought in the whole group.

'One particular memory stands out for me. He was talking about the criticism we'd received after we'd lost a match. This was pretty harsh, and so he talked about our relationship with the press and how we should react to the criticisms: "I don't read what they write about us when things are going badly. I don't let myself be influenced by what they might say, and only read the press when things are going well." He liked positive thinking and the fact that it gives you more energy.

'He was also the first manager who talked to us about the incredibly complicated relationship there can be with criticism: the pressure, the repercussions and how to manage them. If you're a professional footballer, you're open to negative comments with every game, but he showed us that we were above all that, that the journalists could say what they liked, we had to concentrate on our job, which was to make progress. [...] I think that the emotional factor, particularly in football, is a very important phenomenon. I think that being confident gives you more freedom, it liberates you, helps you have the courage to do things on the football pitch. You have to feel free enough to do what your body is telling you to do. Sometimes though, the pressure of winning and the fear of defeat limit your performance. I used to talk about that with Unai and Carcedo because I needed to. Their positive attitude, even at the most difficult moments, meant that the players felt more relaxed on the pitch. And that's what I found personally.'

A positive experience at Valencia

'Unai helped me grasp the importance of the psychological aspect of professional sport, to value the importance of every set piece and strategy that could define a game. And he developed my ability to adapt to different positions, and that made me a better footballer.

I was also lucky enough to arrive in a dressing room that accepted me, with older players who had lots of experience, and younger ones like me… [*he pauses*] I played in attack with Villa and Silva. I profited a lot from that and learnt a lot from them. For a young player like me, what I experienced at Valencia was fantastic.'

11

THE LAND OF THE SHADOWS

'Time flies, doesn't it?' Iñaki Bea has a mischievous look in his eye. The ex-Lorca defender has 'closely followed Unai's progress,' and stayed in contact with him. 'He impressed me because everything happened so quickly… he could have lost control of his career, of himself. But no, he continued his journey to the top without ever slipping back.'

Between his debut on 9 January 2005 in the depths of the *Segunda B* at the Estadio San Pedro in Écija, and his first game in the Champions League on 14 September 2010 at Bursaspor (a 4-0 victory) only five and a half years had passed! 'It's unusual for someone to fully achieve what they set out to do, but you have to put everything into it. It was all down to him,' says Alberto Benito, well aware that people pursue their dreams without really having the capacity to fulfil them, preferring to give up and mutter from behind their computer screens that the big-eared cup or the G-spot don't really exist.

'We played together at Toledo and used to drive to Madrid to watch Real and Atlético training sessions, sometimes in secret. On Sunday, we would go to the games at Rayo Vallecano or other Madrid clubs. Unai has always loved football and all its components, but he educated himself way beyond that, teaching himself all the time. He studied at the Johan Cruyff university, began to consult a psychologist while reading loads of books on the subject of leadership and group management [...] This offered him ways of dealing with pressure, and even of enjoying it. Unai as manager has nothing to do with Unai as player. There was a transformation.'

During his fourth season with Valencia, both sides knew that would be it. Third place in *La Liga* and qualification for the Champions League, as Manuel Llorente and Unai had agreed the previous summer, set the seal on his adventure. 'He fulfilled his contracts at Lorca, Almería and Valencia. How many managers stay until the end of their contract?' asks Francisco, the boy from Almería who in 2011 became the manager of their reserve team in *Segunda B*. 'That says a lot about a manager, his mental strength and his perseverance.' In modern-day football, to spend four years in the same club is rare for a manager. It's well-nigh a myth, or at least a story from the last century, such as that of the brilliant Alfredo Di Stefano (who managed at the Mestalla from 1970 to 1974), of the celebrated Jacinto Quincoces[15] and the Czech Antonín Fivébr, the first trainer in the club's history. No other manager lasted four consecutive seasons apart from Emery, who was also in charge for the greatest number of matches [222].

'When you look at the club's performance after him [5th, 8th, 4th and 12th] you realize even more clearly what Unai achieved. As a supporter, I miss him, and I don't think I'm the only one,' says Juan Sánchez, the man who brought him to Valencia in the first place, and his regular opponent on the local tennis courts.

This gratitude, however, does not extend to the way the Basque trainer left the club, to be replaced by Manuel Pellegrino, a former winner of the UEFA Cup with Valencia who learnt the trade with Benitez at Liverpool and Inter-Milan. A win in the penultimate game at home against Villarreal (1-0), the local rival, produced relief rather than celebration, with the end in sight. Symbolically, Emery's last match was at home – his home – at the Anoeta stadium that saw him grow to manhood. 'Real Sociedad had already been in touch with him and made him a serious offer,' his brother Igor explains. It was

---

15 A former international, Quincoces trained Valencia from 1948 to 1954, and then from 1958 to 1960, while still pursuing a career as an actor.

a tempting offer from a club seeking to restore its glory after several lacklustre seasons and a quick return to the *Segunda*, but Unai had other plans.

'I wanted to leave Spain and test myself in another championship, another country.' A few days before the final game in *La Liga*, Unai agreed to join Spartak Moscow for the next three seasons. He was attracted by the ambitions and resources of the club's owner Leonid Fedun, a Russian businessman with successful investments in the oil and finance industries.[16] Igor for one sees the signing of the contract as surprising and hasty, particularly when he remembers that 'AS Roma expressed an interest in him just before he signed for Moscow...'

Spartak Moscow had just come second in the Russian league and had qualified for the play-off rounds of the Champions League. It is widely considered the most popular club in Russia. Even someone like Alexis Prokopiev, chairman of Russie-Libertés, a human rights and freedom association based in France, can see why: 'I fell in love with the club when I was six. My first visit to the stadium was in a rainstorm. There was no roof and wooden seats, so we all got drenched. It was horrible, above all because the pitch was unplayable. I can't really remember the game or the opposing team, but I haven't forgotten the fervour. The entire crowd stayed through the storm to sing and support their club. It was so rare to see people so joyous in the USSR at that time...'

Born in Moscow in 1983, Alexis left for France at the age of 12, but he hasn't forgotten a thing about his country or its capital, 'a state within the state', he says with a laugh. 'Football was a way of getting together among friends, without seeing or judging any differences. Between 1991 and 1993, when we could see tanks on the streets from our windows, you can't imagine how happy those moments made us feel. In 1993, when there was an attempted putsch, we were forbidden to go to school because it was too dangerous. With my mates we used

---

16 Leonid Fedun is chairman of the IFD Kapital Group, which operates in investment banking and brokerage services. The company was originally underwritten by LUKoil and its two main owners are also the oil company's deputy chief executive Fedun and its CEO Vagit Alekperov.

to go to a small field next to the school and play football all day long. It was a way of escaping from daily reality. Spartak was that as well, of course.'

Spartak above all, according to nostalgic Russians. 'Legend has it that the club was created in the courtyard of a tenement building in Moscow, and that's true to a certain extent,' continues the co-author of the book *Les Autres Visages de la Russie*. 'The team was formed by the grass roots. It was financed by the trade unions, especially those in commerce, and by workmen. It was the opposite of Dynamo, the police club; CSKA, the club of the armed forces, and Torpedo, which was linked to Zil, a big construction company at the start of the 20th century. Unlike them, Spartak is the club of the people, and it's also the most popular. Even today, despite all the difficulties, it's still well supported, at home and even far from Moscow.'

Merely mentioning the name Spartak produces this enthusiasm. 'Let's just say there's a surprising passion for the club,' says Dmitri Popov, the sporting director since 2007. This former international is a discreet man, as was his footballing career, spent between Russia, Israel and Spain, where he was the teammate of a certain Unai Emery at Toledo in 1999. 'He was a very committed lad, a real team player with whom I never had any problem, quite the opposite.'

In spring 2012, Popov was trying to find a new direction for Spartak, headed at the time by Valeri Karpin, managing director and substitute team coach after the departure of Michael Laudrup more than two years earlier. The press attributed Emery's arrival to Karpin, whose years in Spain had been a huge success, especially at Real Sociedad. 'I used to organise my team around him. I've managed good people, less good ones, and some gentlemen. Valeri was one of the last group,' is the praise he wins from Raynald Denoueix, his manager in the days when the Basque team rubbed shoulders with Real Madrid at the top of *La Liga*.

But despite appearances, Unai's arrival in Moscow had nothing to do with Karpin. 'I was the one who suggested him to the owner of Spartak,' says Popov. 'He had shown he was a very good trainer at Valencia by managing to have them always qualify for the Champions League when he didn't have... Let's just say his players were clearly less good than those of Barça and Real, and no better than that of the other clubs. Also, Spartak's philosophy has always been one of attacking football, and so I thought he was the one to be our manager.'

The decision didn't exactly please everyone. 'Karpin's contract as coach had come to an end, but he was still the general manager. I think it had always been his dream to be the permanent manager of Spartak, not just the fill-in one. He immediately set himself apart and was jealous of Unai because he couldn't understand why we appointed him.' This was the start of a latent tension, according to Emery. 'Right from the first day, Karpin didn't want me there. He wanted to be the manager, and so he turned against me. It's as simple as that.' The season hadn't even begun, but it already seemed there would be fireworks, on and off the pitch.

12

THE SPY WHO PLAYED FOR SPARTAK

Like most of the top-flight Russian clubs, Spartak had become international over the previous decade. Under Karpin, there were already three Brazilians in the team (Rafael Carioca, Ari, Welliton), two Argentines (Marcos Rojo and Nicolas Pareja), a Spaniard (Rodri), the Irishman Aiden McGeady and the Dutch player Demy de Zeeuw. After Rojo and Rodri's departures in the summer of 2012, Emery wanted to sign several well-known players. 'I was promised a really talented team. That's why I came here,' he said at the time. Feelers were put out for Bruno Soriano, a defensive playmaker at Villarreal. 'We had lots of meetings in Karpin's office about potential recruits to enable us to compete in the Champions League,' says Mikel Jauregi, who joined the staff together with Juan Carlos Carcedo. Meeting followed meeting, but the promised recruits never arrived, apart from Rômulo, the rising Brazilian star from Vasco da Gama, signed for more than 8 million euros. 'Unai didn't know much about him, but Karpin was convinced about his talent. Unfortunately, he picked up a bad knee injury in September. That was no reflection on his ability – my brother wanted to sign him for Seville years later,' Igor explains. The other new recruits were definitely good players, but not the sort who could change the destiny of a match like certain stars in the Russian championship at that time such as Samuel Eto'o (Anzhi) or Keisuke Honda (CSKA). Other new arrivals were

Kim Källström from Lyons, whom Unai regarded highly both as a
player and a human being, José Manuel Jurado from Schalke, and
the Argentine defender Juan Manuel Insaurralde from Boca Juniors:
someone definitely chosen by Karpin, because Emery had to watch
videos of him after he had arrived at the club. 'We had the resources
to do something in a difficult championship, but I soon saw there
were better teams than us…'

Still confident, Unai immediately introduced principles already
tried and tested in Spain. Once again, this proved too hasty. 'We
made mistakes, but then, who hasn't? We had to get used to their
footballing customs, to their way of working. And to do that we had
to learn the Russian language. We tried, but it was very complicated,'
Carcedo explains.

Strangely enough, the Russian classes weren't organised by Spartak,
but by someone from outside the club, Evgeniya Larioshkina. 'I didn't
work for Spartak, but I used to spend half the year in Gipuzkoa,
Unai's homeland,' she says, referring to the fact that her partner was
a native of Irun. 'I knew that Unai was going to work at Spartak, a
team I support even though as a journalist I have to be objective
[laughter]. So, I wrote to him, he replied, and that's how we started to
work together.' Several times a week, Emery met Evgeniya to learn
the language from scratch. 'Even if you have several classes a week,
you need months to reach a decent level. Unai worked so hard in
training and preparing for games that time for learning the language
was rather limited. I based my classes around words linked to football.
I discussed tactics and systems explaining the key words he would
need to use in his job. Since I was as crazy as him about football, we
could spend hours talking about players or games, without seeing the
time pass.'

Despite this, Unai made little progress, and this annoyed certain
people at Spartak. 'At first he found it really hard. Unai can be
criticised for many things, but when he does something, he does it
with all his heart. Even when it came to learning Russian, he was
always highly motivated even though he had great difficulties. He
insisted on learning English as well so that he could have a better

dialogue with the players. In fact, gradually we learnt more English than Russian,' explains Evgeniya.

The linguistic difficulties ran into another unexpected obstacle. 'The club's interpreter sometimes found it hard to translate the idea that Unai was trying to transmit. A lot of Spanish expressions make no sense if they're translated literally into Russian, and vice-versa. That gave rise to lots of problems,' agrees Jauregi, whose job was to analyse the matches. 'Three of us worked on the videos. We isolated images of our opponents in order to make a defensive, offensive, strategic but also individual montage of every opposing player. After we edited the video, Unai gave them the finishing touches, then delivered his messages to the squad. For every game, he studied six or seven matches that the other team had played. Our idea was to show our left-winger the movements of the opposing right-back, his ten or eleven most frequent actions, so that he wouldn't be taken by surprise if that player had the habit of cutting inside or of trying to go around someone on the right.'

This meticulous preparation wasn't necessarily suited to the new environment in Moscow. 'Every country has their own way of working. It's just a different methodology, it doesn't mean they're better or worse. Our big mistake was not to adapt to this cultural difference and their way of doing things. The things we were in the habit of doing, whether it was using videos or the time of day when we worked, were not in their customs. We should have introduced the details of our methodology bit by bit.'

This self-criticism could seem a little harsh given the start Spartak had to the season. 'We won our first four games, if I remember rightly [in fact, it was three]. Then, above all, came the match with Fenerbahçe, the one we had to win,' recalls Popov. This was a play-off for the group stage of the Champions League, Muscovites' main goal for the season and the 'reason that Unai was brought in,' says Alexis Prokopiev. 'We played a great game in the first leg in Moscow, winning 2-1. At times, it seemed like a return to the typical Spartak style of play. Short passes, always going forward, and then calmer periods, as in the days of Alenichev.'[17] Without the same brilliance, of course, but a 1-1 draw in Istanbul proved sufficiently solid to qualify 3-2 on aggregate to join Barcelona, Benfica and Celtic in Group G that autumn.

It seemed everything was for the best in the best of possible worlds... 'It's true Unai got off on the right foot,' Dmitri Popov admits. But the seeds of doubt had already been sown in a 5-0 defeat at Zenit. 'The Russian championship isn't as easy as people think. With the European games, we were playing twice a week but didn't get good results. Then things started snowballing...'

The metaphor makes sense. Week after week Spartak's inconsistency grew. Kirill Kombarov, a frequent substitute, seemed to have a negative influence on his brother Dmitri because of his clumsiness. The poor left-back, a regular for both club and country, even scored an own goal against Celtic in the second game of the Champions League. The Hoops won 3-2, helped by the sending-off of Insaurralde, and ending a series of 19 consecutive matches when they hadn't won an away game in the competition... 'The trainer, the players, the president, the managing director, myself, everyone: we should have sat down round a table and speak openly to one another. If Unai didn't succeed here, it's because we didn't do that,' Popov believes.

The people's club was not left far behind in the championship (fifth place) but it lost the decisive encounters: 1-2 at Lokomotiv, 0-2 against CSKA, 1-2 at Anzhi Makhachkala, including an own goal in the 92nd minute by the long-suffering Insaurralde, and a humiliation at home against Dinamo, (1-5). 'Unai didn't understand the Russian mentality. He was used to a certain way of behaving and of living with the players and the media, but all that's different here,' according to Spartak's sporting director, who adds several concrete examples. 'He was too generous with the players, far too generous! There was a lack of discipline, the training sessions weren't taken seriously. He let them off without a fine because sometimes he was the one at fault. One day,

---

17 Dimitri Alenichev was an attacking midfielder in the great Spartak team of the 1990s, when they were Russian champions four times. He trained the 'red and whites' during the 2015-16 season.

we were travelling for the championship, and one of the players had forgotten his passport. You need one in Russia even for internal flights.

'Because we were Spartak there wasn't a problem, but Unai shouted at the player in front of all the others. "Forgetting your passport means you aren't thinking of the team. It's a lack of respect towards your teammates, blah blah blah!" Less than a week later, we were going to Benfica, which meant an international flight. And the only one who forgot his passport was… Unai. The whole team had to wait three hours for him to get it so that we could leave. There was a difference between what he said and what he did, and so gradually the players lost their respect for him.'

The dressing room soon became a minefield, especially when Emery left Artem Dyzuba on the bench. 'I had arguments with him. He was in the national side as well and had a great influence over the journalists because he talked to them a lot. So did some of the other Spartak players,' Unai remembers. 'I began to feel isolated. Completely on my own. Karpin didn't help me in the slightest. Once he called a meeting and began to attack my staff. I defended them and asked him why he was doing that. From then on, we had a real falling-out. [*He pauses*] On the one hand, I had Karpin doing all he could to make my life impossible. On the other there was Dyzuba stirring up the players and the journalists against me as soon as I played him less. I found myself all alone, without the possibility of doing anything.'

The upshot: following the hammering against Dinamo on 25 November, Unai was sacked, only six months after his appointment. 'Karpin made the announcement directly to the journalists, who applauded him! It was surreal! The fact is, I should never have come here. I was taken in by the plan they sold me and fell into a club where nobody helped me. When I left, I said the main problem had been the language. I said that to avoid trouble, because I know that certain clubs are dangerous. If anybody doesn't believe me, just ask Dmitri Popov or the club president, who was the only one who really supported me.'

Whereas Fedun and Karpin didn't want to speak, Popov confirms most of what Emery says: 'Above all, Unai is intelligent. He was clumsy at Spartak, but I'm sure he learnt from his mistakes, and I'm glad about that. As far as training, methodology, taking training, exercise and tactic sessions are concerned, I think he's one of the very best. I insist, one of the very best. But he lost control of the dressing room; I told him so on several occasions. During training, two foreign players were spotted in the early hours at a hotel with girls. Everybody was aware of it. Unai called them in but didn't punish them and pardoned them. Like it or not, if you let a player off like that, he begins to behave differently…'

When it comes down to it though, it's not these mistakes, or the photos of Unai with his girlfriend in a restaurant only a few hours after the defeat to CSKA, that are the real problem. 'He never considered a player's status. He has always worked on merit and the collective performance,' says Jauregi. 'But how can you square that meritocracy with the rule stipulating that there must be a minimum of four Russian players on the pitch?[18] 'I've often wondered about Emery as the Spartak coach,' Dyzuba told Russian Eurosport. 'For him, the best player was Demy de Zeeuw […] The strong, talented Russian players were left on the bench and hardly ever entered the pitch. It was the foreigners who played. And what about Spartak's young players? Emery took almost all the young players out of the team. Personally, I don't understand.'

If nobody understood how poorly Dzyuba performed at Euro 16 or for Spartak, so poorly that the club's bright young star was sold to Zenit, his bitterness is symptomatic of Unai's stay at the club, surrounded by intrigue. 'With hindsight, many supporters wonder why Karpin didn't do more,' Prokopiev suggests. 'He let the situation grow worse and worked on the team on his own account. That didn't calm things down, but it reassured some people. Karpin never smiles, and publicly criticises the players. Emery always gave a positive message to the press, which isn't part of Russian culture. Here, a trainer has to show suffering and authority. Psychology often gets forgotten.'

---

18 According to new legislation, there now have to be five Russian players on the field.

Spartak finished the season in fourth place, and Karpin himself was sacked the following year, above all after being eliminated from the Russian Cup when they were beaten by FC Tosno, a team from the Russian third division. His three successors, Dmitri Gunko, Murat Yakin and Alenichev, were not much more successful: finishing sixth, sixth and fifth in successive years. However, little by little, thanks to Popov's growing influence and the departure of Roman Askhabadze, a man from the shadows promoted to managing director after Karpin took over as trainer once more, the club calmed down and managed to drive away the circling vultures. With some degree of success, even if rumour has it that a visitor still has to hand over his passport at the entrance 'in order to make a photocopy, just in case there's trouble...' Doubtless this is nothing more than gossip, adding to the folklore linked to the people of Moscow's true club.

'Our team has really suffered, and its red and white colours suit it because they're the symbols of blood,' says Prokopiev, basing this on many works in Russian as well as the excellent book in English by Robert Edelman, *A History of the People's Team in the Workers' State*, which tells a fascinating story. 'After 1953, Spartak was protected by the upper echelons of the Communist party, but still had many scars from Stalinism. Its founders spent 12 years in the camps. The father of the club's top goalscorer (Nikita Simonyan, who scored 160 goals) was put in prison in an attempt to force his son to be transferred to Dinamo Tbilisi.' Another star (Sergei Sal'nikov) was forced to move to city rival's Dinamo. His stepfather had been arrested and imprisoned for financial crimes. Sal'nikov received a message from the police saying that he would most likely die in prison that winter but that his conditions would be considerably improved if the player moved to Dinamo, which he did in 1949. 'Then there's also the story of the captain's brother, who is still in the camps.'

These are undeniable facts, even if Spartak fans are accused of always exaggerating, of turning history into myth, as with the autobiography of the English player Jim Riordan, *The Spy Who Played for Spartak*, who claims to have played for the red and whites while there's no trace of him in the club's archives... That's precisely the problem with Spartak, everyone has their own version of events:

Karpin, Popov, Emery, who to believe? None of them and all of them: nobody is a mind-reader.

When he returned to his apartment in the evening, or when he relaxed for a while in a restaurant, Unai often looked over his shoulder, feeling as if somebody were spying on him from a distance. Was it paranoia or confirmation that 'certain clubs can be dangerous?' It's said that Riordan's official date of death was 10 February 2012, but who knows? A spy never dies, at least not until his secrets are out in the open. Until then, as in every Russian tale, his shadow pursues you: in dark streets or alleyways, but above all, in your mind.

13

REKINDLING THE FLAME

Early in 2013, at the Hotel Meliá Valencia, an out-of-the-way four-star hotel near the centre of the city, ideal for a business meeting, Unai Emery waits patiently in a private room with his agent, Iñaki Ibáñez. After refusing an approach from Espanyol, the Basque trainer has agreed to meet Seville's sporting director, Monchi, who was anxious to change things after their defeat against Valencia, the fifth in their last seven encounters in *La Liga*. An agreement is quickly reached for a year-and-a-half contract, but the discussions extend to six hours in talks about the squad, their aims and football in general. 'We forgot about time,' Monchi has often joked when describing this meeting to journalist friends like Roberto Arrocha (*ABC*), the co-author of his biography: *Monchi. León de San Fernando.* As he was saying goodbye to his future manager, Monchi posed him one final question: 'If we work hand in hand for the next two years, where do you think Seville will be?' 'Champions', replied Emery.

This is a word clearly showing Emery's famous *mentalidad ganadora*. Despite his first failure, his first sacking, his first period without a club, Emery was convinced he had gained enough experience to help him, both as regards sport and as a human being, as with every challenge he faced. Pablo Rodriguez, his 'rival on the left in the days when we played for Ferrol', confirms this with an example: 'When at

Ferrol the club bosses told him he wasn't being kept on, he took that very well. His first reaction was to thank everyone for what he had learnt here. He didn't try to argue but capitalised on the experience to move on.'

Ten years later, Unai still had the same idea, with just one slight nuance: the presence of Juan Carlos Carcedo. 'Spartak was fundamental in our journey because we came up against something new.

It helped us in the way we treated players, to have an even more psychological approach. Almost every day, Unai and I exchange ideas about every player: how to deal with him, how to behave to get the best out of him. That sometimes means giving him a dressing-down in front of everyone, but then you have to anticipate the possible reaction. With some players, it's best to have the talk in private, in the privacy of an office, with no one looking on. Every player is like a new world; you have to press the right button to get inside him, work out his weak points, his strengths and what he's thinking.'

On 14 January 2013, Unai and Juan Carlos were presented to the squad as replacements for Míchel, who had been there less than a year. 'It really wasn't easy,' remembers Andrés Palop, the legendary goalkeeper who had arrived in 2005 and had twice won the Copa del Rey and the UEFA Cup together with Frédéric Kanouté, Julien Escudé, Daniel Alves, Luis Fabiano and the sadly missed Antonio Puerta. 'After being through all that, it's difficult to start a season with only moderate results and increasing problems in the dressing room.' The reason: a tired squad with no less than eleven nationalities and a shocking lack of cohesion, according to the right-back Coke. 'During my first season at Seville, the previous year, I played quite a lot. But that year I no longer played at all. Several players were in the same situation as me, a bit lost, as if the group was split.'

It was a situation described by Emery a few years later in an interview with *El País* newspaper: 'The team was in tatters [...] The two captains didn't speak to each other, they saw one another as rivals. Spahic was seen as half-crazy, and it was said that Reyes was burnt-out.' Added to that was the fact the knee injury of Piotr Trochowski, the German international attacking midfielder had at first been misdiagnosed, which led to an operation that ruined his season and eventually his whole career… Cala, a defender who came up through the ranks at the club, sums up this period clearly and simply: 'Everything was going badly. The team had some good players, but it didn't hold together. It didn't hold together…' It didn't matter that Seville had players such as Ivan Rakitic, Gary Medel, Cicinho or Diego Perotti, the club would never get back into Europe without greater cohesion, a new mindset.

'Unai wanted to rebuild team spirit, because there had been some real rows on the training pitch,' Palop explains. 'So he took us out of the training environment. Sometimes we didn't play football but went for bike rides or went karting. He tried to make us have a laugh together, to get to know one another, to eat together.' Full-time manager, entertainment organiser, occasional compere, Emery employed the same methods as during his early days at Valencia: rekindling the flame of his players, their passion for football. 'He gave me back my enthusiasm, my motivation. It was as if I had rediscovered my desire to compete at the highest level. At every moment he conveyed a love of football so that we could go out onto the pitch and live it. The way he patrolled the technical area, his concentration, his vision… Sincerely, during his pre-match talks or the discussions at the start of the week about our upcoming opponents, he inspired us in a way that meant we did what he wanted on the pitch,' adds the goalkeeper, backed up by Coke. 'As with each change of manager, everybody starts again from scratch and wants to show he's worthy of being picked. That's normal. But with Unai there was more than that. I think every player had a "before" and "after" Unai that year…'

The first of June, the last day of the *Liga*. Almost six months have gone by, but the team from Andalusia has not climbed up the table, due mainly to a remarkable inconsistency: unbeatable in their Sánchez-Pizjuán stadium (3-0 against Grenada, 4-1 against Celta Vigo and 4-0 against Zaragoza) but dreadful away from home (1-4 against Real Madrid, 1-2 at Mallorca, 0-1 at Levante…), a feature of Emery's years at Seville. There was still a hope though that they could be in the Europa Cup, because the two other clubs in contention, Málaga and Rayo Vallecano, faced the threat of being excluded from European competitions by UEFA due to their debts. This would free up two places for the Europa League and allow Seville to sneak in by the back door. A kind of miracle, although you had to have faith to believe in it. 'From the very first day, Unai was convinced we would qualify. His talk before the last match insisted on the need to win so that we could compete in the Europa League the next season. He had no doubt about it,' says Alvaro Negredo.

Emery was confident: he knew fate wouldn't betray him. It never had done, either in the land of his father and grandfather for the play-offs to get into *Segunda*, or in the stormy arena of Almería, when defeat by Cádiz could have led to him being sacked after only four games. It had to be with him today, especially against such an adversary: Valencia.

They also had an advantage over Real Sociedad for fourth place and qualification for the qualifying round of the Champions League. Both teams therefore absolutely needed to win, in a context made even more special because it was the last game for local boy Jesús Navas, and for Negredo, both moving to Manchester City. 'Seville is a club and a city I am very fond of. Those were the best years of my footballing career, four years I won't forget,' says Negredo, whose reunion with Emery led to his best season (31 goals). Another player leaving the club after the game was Andrés Palop, who was close to 40 years old and had played 294 games in all competitions for the *Nervionesnes*. 'We won titles and the people of Seville were always grateful to us for that. But on our side, we also showed them day after day all the passion we felt for the club. I don't want to sound bitter, but I'm one of those from another era. I'm not the kind of player who gets tattoos all over his body, who dyes his hair to have a photo taken, and couldn't care less what club he plays for. We really lived the successes we had and shared them with the supporters. That was what made my eight years there so intense and beautiful.'

The goalie intended to prolong the pleasure of playing football with a further year at Bayer Leverkusen, but not before he had a proper sending off from 'the fans, the club, and the city' which had made him feel at home. 'The problem was that I got injured two or three weeks before Unai arrived.

Beto was brought in on loan, and he became the first choice. In the week leading up to the game against Valencia, I heard rumours that I might play, but I hadn't been picked for two months and it was crucial that we won if we wanted to play in the Europa League. Unai said nothing special to me, we just carried on working as normal. Then when match day came around, I was surprised to find not only was I in the starting eleven, but he had made me captain... [*A long pause*] That's something I'll never forget. He realised everything I had achieved here, and he allowed me to finish in the Sánchez-Pizjuán stadium one last time. That was all I could ask for.'

Palop went onto the pitch with his two sons, Jorge and Alejandro. In the stands, a huge banner was unfurled with two words on it in the language of Valencia, his native region: it read *Gràcies Capità*. Lots of emotion, but the tears could wait. The visitors' Ever Banega sent a shot rocketing into the net after only eleven minutes, followed by another one against the bar from Roberto Soldado. Seville was on the ropes, but one man was determined to leave with his head held high: Alvaro Negredo. 'I don't know if it was chance, or destiny... but it was a crazy game. Completely crazy. At the end of a poor season, we managed to qualify for the Europa League by winning 4-3 against Valencia, who lost the fourth spot. And I scored all four goals! Honestly, is there a better way to leave a club?' A scissor kick, a penalty, and two perfect strikes from centres: Negredo could leave feeling proud of himself, and Palop was carried off the pitch in triumph.

Emery was happy too, even if he had to nervously await UEFA's verdict on Málaga and Rayo Vallecano. His destiny though knew that this match would change his life. It didn't tell him so yet, however, because it was too busy haunting Valencia, who lost out on the Champions League to Real Sociedad and had to fall back on the Europa League, the competition Seville also joined a few weeks later, for the preliminary rounds. But from there to imagine a semi-final between the two teams the following May in the stifling heat of the Mestalla stadium you would have to be a screenplay writer in Hollywood or the desert of Tabernas. Even then, Sergio Leone would have told you the story was too fantastic to be true to life...

14

CONQUERING EUROPE

Mladost Podgorica, Slask Wroclaw, Estoril, Freiburg, Slovan Liberec, Maribor, Betis and Porto. The teams in the campaign for the Europa League 2013-14 were an invitation to dream, to travel, from Montenegro to Slovenia by way of a Seville derby in a dramatic quarter-final worthy of the opera *Carmen*. In the first leg, Betis had won 2-0 at Sánchez-Pizjuán, leaving the Seville club little hope of a *remontada*. 'The next day, all the team was down, but Unai gave us a talk the leitmotif of which was: "Forget about that game, because I know we can beat them!" He convinced us all we could do it,' says Coke. 'What's good about Unai is that he knows how to treat each game differently. However important the game against Betis was, he placed just as much weight on the following game. That Sunday, we were playing in *La Liga* and were thinking only of that. His way of valuing every competition, including the Copa del Rey, is good for the whole group.'

That Sunday, Valladolid were beaten 4-1. Four days later, and Betis were eliminated on penalties (2-2 on aggregate, 4-3 on penalties to Seville), despite the fact that Vitolo missed the first *rojiblanco* penalty. 'Unai is capable of giving you a confidence, a motivation, even an anger that certain trainers would never be able to get out of you,' in the opinion of the Seville winger, who had arrived that summer from Las Palmas. 'I was playing in the *Segunda*, nobody in the *Liga* knew me. But from the first game, he put me in the starting line-up. I'll remember that all my life!'

That having been said, the start of that season had been a torture: three defeats, two draws and one off the bottom of the table! Seville did manage to defeat Rayo Vallecano (4-1) and shared the points with Real Sociedad (1-1), but the game at home against Almería on the eighth day could have been fatal for Emery if they had lost. 'He was going through a difficult time, but so were we,' recalls Francisco, Unai's striker during his first year with Almería, who by now had become the trainer of the first team. 'Seville was still among the clubs that could be relegated, and we were drawing 1-1 with them, away. Then in the 92nd minute Rakitic made it 2-1, and that was it for us, because shortly afterwards the ref blew his whistle. I felt bad about it for a while, but in the end I was pleased because that breathed life back into Unai and Seville. After that match, they began to win. Cruel luck for Francisco – who did, however, succeed brilliantly in keeping his side up despite ten defeats in the championship – but a lifeline for Emery.

'We got our style of play wrong,' says Cala, who left that winter for Cardiff after playing on 19 occasions in the first half of the season. 'Unai asked us how we saw the team, how we could improve it. If you disagreed with him, you could say so, because he never took any reprisals. It's been different with some managers I've known, they would drop you if you dared say anything they didn't like. It wasn't like that with Unai. He always asked us to argue, and that led to a debate: "I don't think that would be a good solution for this, this and this. Why do you think it would be good?" You felt you were important because he took your view into account.'

Thanks to a big reshuffle halfway through the year, with the arrival of Vitolo, Vicente Iborra, Carlos Bacca, Kevin Gameiro (who should have joined Unai at Valencia), Sébastian Cristoforo, Diogo Figueiras as well as many loans (Stéphane M'Bia, Nicolas Pareja, Marko Marin, Daniel Carriço and Denis Cheryshev), all Seville needed was time. There was no lack of talent, in fact there was almost too much of it and that upset the balance of the team as a whole. 'At first, I wanted to use Rakitic as part of a two-man midfield so that he could have the ball in front of him. We did create chances, but we suffered when we lost the ball, because there was too big a gap between midfield and defence, a lack of cover. So I decided to add a second defensive midfielder and to put Rakitic higher up the field, even if to begin with he wasn't happy about receiving the ball with his back to the goal from time to time. But we needed more stability, and that also allowed him to be closer to the goal. I believe in allowing creative players to express themselves. They're the ones people go to the games to see,' explains Emery, who from this point on employed his Seville trademark, the *doble pivote*, in other words, the combination of two defensive midfielders. 'We did that occasionally at Valencia, but we developed it here,' Carcedo adds. 'At those difficult moments we reinforced our defence, but that didn't mean we abandoned our attacking approach, because we've always liked that. It's all a question of degree. We put in place strategies for when the team was suffering, and others for the moments when it needed to attack and make our opponents soak up the pressure, which can't last a whole match. These pivots were central to all the covering the team did, especially the backs when they came into play. As we see it, backs have always been important to launch attacks and even score goals. In order to give them that freedom, the pivot players have to lose some of theirs so that they can provide cover at the right moment.'

It was an evolution in the game, as well as in Emery's mentality, 'a trainer who found it a bit hard to control his wish to win by always scoring more,' says Negredo, referring to their year in the *Liga* with Almería. 'He learnt from experience at Seville. During the training sessions, we were completely focused on our next opponents, because you don't play the same way against Barça or Real Madrid as you do against other teams. Unai was even more obsessed with every detail than before. But he was calmer as well. He had learnt that you could win only 1-0, that this also brought you three points as well [*laughs*]. He wanted us to control the rhythm of play, to pass the ball from one side of the pitch to the other if we were winning, not always to press forward to score another goal, running the risk of a counter-attack and ending up with a draw.'

More measured, more rational, Unai was learning with age, and also thanks to the growing influence of his assistant, Carcedo, praised by everyone in Almería and Valencia, for example Sofiane Feghouli: 'They complement each other perfectly. Before a game, Unai paces up and down the dressing room nervously, coffee in hand; then Carcedo arrives and cracks jokes. It's the same in training, each has their own role. It's the best duo I've ever known.' Cala, who reckons to 'have learnt to defend better thanks to Carcedo,' also mentions this man in the shadows as Emery's 'life support'. 'He has changed his physio and lots of other things during his career, but never his assistant manager. That tells you everything.'

This loyalty flatters the person in question, whose beliefs have never changed: work, a word he repeats tirelessly, and learning, especially from his masters. 'I knew Arrigo Sacchi at Atlético Madrid. He was a maestro.[19] He knew how to keep the line of the back four while teaching us to communicate with each other. The Italians do that very well in defence. I also knew Sandro Salvioni at Nice and we worked nearly every day on our defensive tactics. Maybe in Spain we prefer to play and keep possession. For example, I've also played for Las Palmas. In the Canary Islands they have a different philosophy from the rest of Spain, where there are several schools of thought depending on the region or club. Perhaps it's because of the climate, perhaps it's due to a different set of circumstances, but down there our game was one of passing, of technique, because many of the local players had started out playing street football, which is very common there. That was what I grew up with. A complete manager shouldn't neglect any aspect of the game, it's not possible.'

If Emery has a reputation for being meticulous, so too does Carcedo. 'He always used to repeat something to me: use your body to defend. Sometimes it was the gap you left to your opponent that you could close by bending your body the right way, or other similar small details,' recalls Coke, who became part of the team's engine room together with Iborra and Vitolo, two Spanish players almost unknown to the public at large, having played respectively at Rayo Vallecano,

---

19 In the Spanish meaning of the term, *maestro* signifies teacher.

Levante and Las Palmas. 'I learnt an enormous amount tactically and defensively, even though I played in a lot of different attacking positions. With those two, you learn to live football, to think football, to be competitive', says Vitolo, whose praise could be seen to have a double meaning: isn't there a risk then if the player isn't really in love with football? 'Let's just say that if the players love the same thing as you, it makes things easier and avoids you making mistakes. Luckily for Unai, we were players who loved the sport, and so...'

Of course, there was still some yawning during the long chats and video sessions, but the squad understood the need for that kind of work. 'There are days when you appreciate it, and others when it gets to you a bit. Personally, I'm one of those who thinks you have to give as much information as possible to a player,' says Cala. 'Unai gives two or three talks in the days before a match. One is about our opponents, the next about us, and on match day he talks about the personal aspect, the team spirit. He tries to touch on the sensitive aspect of each player before the warm-up. We'd done all the tactical preparation during the week, and he had mentioned it the day before: the way our opponents played, what kind of mistakes they made, how we had to catch them out...'

These demands were the more easily accepted, according to the young Seville player, because Emery 'was always the first to arrive at the *Ciudad Deportiva* [training ground] and the last to leave. He worked almost 24 hours a day! When he demanded something of you, you were aware he demanded ten times more of himself. His dedication pushed you to give more.' All of which obviously didn't prevent rows or shouting matches during training sessions, particularly with one of the new summer recruits, the Colombian striker Carlos Bacca. 'He had lots of very loud arguments with him,' Igor says with a smile. 'Bacca even insulted him, and yet he's the first to be pleased for him nowadays!'

This is a difficult moment for a manager, one that Unai had already experienced at Valencia with a French player, Tino Costa. 'I've always liked to have good relations with my players, but sometimes things get out of hand,' admits Emery. 'That happened to me twice, with Costa at Valencia and Bacca at Seville. Both times they came on in the second half and played very badly. In the dressing room, I was angry with Tino: "You came onto the pitch without committing yourself, with no respect for the club or your teammates!" If I have to call a spade a spade, I do so. If I have to have a confrontation with a player, it doesn't bother me, I'll argue face to face. With Bacca it was the same. He came on and played very badly in a home game, and afterwards, in the dressing room... The next day we discussed things calmly, without the irritation of the previous evening. I don't hold grudges. What matters at moments like those is the respect the player should have for his teammates, the staff – myself included – and the entire club.'

Being pardoned like that was something Bacca must have understood, because he never forgets to thank God whenever he scores a goal or talks to the press. 'At twenty, I was working in my village, Puerto Colombia, as an assistant on a bus. Then I had to work as a ticket inspector because I was from a poor family and needed to earn money to help them. The doors to football stayed shut to me for a long time, and by then I thought I couldn't count on it any more. But that year I had a trial for Junior de Barranquilla, and thanks be to God, they took me on,' he told *Marca*. After also being a fisherman in his early years, it wasn't until 26 that he reached Europe, signing for Club Brugge in Belgium, after an impressive period in Barranquilla and a spell on loan at Minervén in Venezuela.

It had been a bumpy road for the young striker, the way that Monchi, the builder of the Seville team, likes his players to arrive. 'It's become impossible to imagine our club without Monchi. He's one of the most important people in our history. Modern-day Seville means Monchi,' says Carlos Moreno, a student of the club's past and legacy, who is full of praise for him. Arriving in 1990, the man whose real name is Ramón Rodríguez Verdejo was in those days a young goalkeeper from the next-door province of Cádiz. He was to remain on the playing staff at Seville for ten years, alongside some great players (Davor Suker, Vasillis Tsartas, Diego Simeone, Diego Maradona) and trainers, from Luis Aragonés to Carlos Bilardo, the man who led Argentina to World Cup victory in 1986.

'He [Bilardo] is the person who had the most influence on me in football and life as a whole,' Monchi told Álvaro Corazón Rural, a journalist for *Jot Down* in 2014. 'Every single detail was taken into account, sometimes to the extreme. He even went way beyond that. For example, the training sessions had to be open to all members of the club, from the stewards to the doctors… His theory was that if one day he fell ill, and the second and third coaches also fell ill, the physio would have to pick the team, so he ought to know how to take the training as well… In our hotels, we used to lounge around in our flip-flops, but Bilardo still kept his boots on. When I asked him why, he replied: "What if the hotel catches fire? What if we all have to run out? You'll be in flip-flops…" He calculated everything. I'm like him in that respect, I like to have everything under control. I worry about things that might seem banal, but that's my idea of football. And I learnt all that from him, because I spent a whole year next on the bench next to him.'

Relegated to the *Segunda* in the 2000-01 season, Monchi was hoping to return to the top flight the following year. But a shoulder injury made that impossible for him, and his career came to an end during the pre-season tour of Holland. 'An adopted son of Seville' as he nicely puts it, his future was already mapped out. The club offered him to be a spokesman, then the press manager, then the travel organiser and finally the post of sporting director, the post he held until his departure in April 2017 to take up a similar job at AS Roma. 'He has a way of talking to you, of presenting things to you… It's very hard to say no to Monchi,' according to Julien Escudé, who spent more than six years in the Andalusian capital, from January 2006 to the summer of 2012. 'He is permanently concerned with the player's well-being, especially the foreign ones. He knows how to build a squad, not simply on the basis of their footballing talent. He used to insist a lot on the mix of personalities, of characters.' The 'lion of San Fernando' – the village where he was born, prefers to talk of 'luck' and praises his network of scouts, which involved more than 15 people working full-time all round the planet, recently joined by Óscar Arias, technical director at Seville since 2013.

Most of Monchi's colleagues and agents say he is 'the best sporting director in the world'. What impresses them are his talents as a negotiator and his instinct for discovering 'gems'. 'I don't always get it right, I've also made choices that didn't come off,' Monchi often insists during interviews, preferring to play down his influence in the two UEFA Cups (2006 and 2007), the European Supercup in 2006, and the two Copa del Rey trophies (2007 and 2010), while waiting for the titles yet to be won thanks to his collaboration with Emery.

This discretion is a compliment applied to somebody who's real passion is… carnival, as with any self-respecting *Gaditano*.[20] A slave to his job, Monchi was the perfect match for Emery, who shares the same ideas about how to play the game and how to develop a team. 'I like to discuss, to have my ideas challenged,' says the manager. 'We often have meetings where I tell him what I need, how I see the players, and he will explain his own ideas. That can take hours, and even if we don't always agree, we make progress. By confronting each other's ideas, it forces us to back up our opinion and to question ourselves.'

This intellectual stimulation is something Unai needs, according to his staff and his former sporting directors. One of these, Roberto Olabe, explains: 'He likes to surround himself with people who force him to evolve. His viewpoint has always been: "I want to improve, I want us all to improve, so be demanding with me, because I'll be demanding of you." To achieve this, he needs different ideas from the ones he has, and he's aware of that.'

To be aware of one's weaknesses, one's qualities and possibilities has been an inner effort that Emery has been making for more than 15 years, one that led him to a Europa League semi-final against Valencia that spring. In spite of himself, he had become the symbol of the *Murciélagos'* hostility towards Seville, a rivalry that is both recent and not really reciprocated. 'Before every game, he likes to go out onto the pitch on his own for a moment, to sniff the atmosphere, look at the stands, think. He's always done that,' says his brother Igor.

---

20 A *Gaditano* is a native of the province of Cádiz, whose carnival is one of the most baroque in Europe.

'For the first leg of the semi-final, away in Valencia, he carried out the same ritual, which he does an hour or an hour and a quarter before kick-off. The Valencia supporters were already in the stands. When they saw him, they started to shout: *"Emery, hijo de puta!"* [Emery, you son of a bitch!] He looked up at them, then went back into the dressing room as normal.' This cool headedness was rewarded with a 2-0 victory, giving Seville a clear advantage for the return game on 1 May.' We had the final almost within our grasp, and then they scored three goals against us,' recalls Coke, who was in the starting line-up that day. Feghouli (14th minute), a Beto own goal (26th) and Mathieu (69th) galvanised the fans, but in the wrong way. 'Our parents arrived and heard the chants and lots of other insults. They were frightened and so watched the game from their hotel bedroom,' recalls Igor. Emery also heard them, but stayed out on the touchline, encouraging his players. 'They were badly affected, some of them dropped their heads. We were losing our dream, so it was up to me to show them I still believed in it. I made some changes, tried not to be passive in the face of events. I still believed, even though the minutes were ticking away.' Seville pressed, but to no avail, until one last throw-in: a set piece that Emery had always worked at painstakingly. 'Except that by this time it was more like "anything goes", there weren't really any tactics, we simply all rushed into the attack', says Coke, who grabbed the ball after a physio had handed it to Unai. Way outside his technical area, the manager signalled all his players to get forward. What followed was out of this world, out of a rational world at least. 'I threw in and Fazio headed it on, then M'Bia ran on to it and scored. In the 94th minute, which meant we qualified for the final!', remembers Coke. 'I don't think I'll ever live through another game like that one. Ever.'

For his part, Emery had already lived through a similar moment, at Irun. He saw himself nine years earlier, running onto the pitch, eyes popping, hugging whoever he met. Apart from the suit, nothing had really changed; 'Football is a feeling. Either you have it or you don't, but it comes from the heart,' he concludes. His heart needed to stay strong, because the final in Turin was less than a fortnight away…

15.1

THE WONDERS OF SEVILLE

More than two years had gone by since Stéphane M'Bia first appeared on the pitch at the Mestalla stadium. Seville continued its fairy tale journey through Europe: Liège, Rotterdam, Rijeka, Mönchengladbach, Saint-Petersburg, Florence, Molde, Basel or Donetsk, the dream never ended, not even in the finals against Benfica (0-0, won 4-2 on penalties), Dnipro (3-2) and Liverpool (3-1). 'Everybody knows what Unai Emery did at Seville. Three consecutive Europa League Cups! But not everyone realizes how big an achievement that was,' says Adil Rami, who came to Andalusia in 2015. Only Giovanni Trapattoni had done something similar in the past, with the UEFA Cup, but his victories were not consecutive. 'The hardest thing in football is to consolidate, to win something for a second time, to motivate yourself again, to respond to expectations. From the outside, you simply have to say: "Bravo!"', stresses Juan Mata.

By now, this gratitude extended far beyond Seville and its fans, who sang their love song to Unai in the second Europa League campaign that was to take them to Warsaw, host city for the final. *Es que yo sin ti, Emery, no podría ser feliz; llévame a Varsovia, llévame a Tbilisi!*[21] (which translates literally as, 'Without you, Emery, I

---

21 Tbilisi is the capital of Georgia and hosted the European Supercup in 2015.

couldn't be happy, take me with you to Warsaw, take me to Tbilisi!')
It was a remix of '*El Perdón*', a song by Nicky Jam and Enrique
Iglesias, invented by two female Seville fans, which quickly went
viral in Spain. 'We shared it on Unai's social media and sent them
two signed shirts,' recalls Igor. 'We tried to take them to Warsaw, but
it was complicated with the flights, and the number of seats we had
[...] That song demonstrates the osmosis of Unai's time at Seville.
That 2014-15 season was perhaps the most beautiful in terms of
our communion with people.'

When the results follow, the life of a player or manager is
beautiful, no matter in what country, city or club. If this good fortune
happens to take place in Seville, then the rewards are infinite. 'For
me, Seville has a special colour, and it's white and red [...] to smell
the perfume of gin and tonic, of camomile; it's the colour of the
trees, of horse-drawn carriages on the Paseo Colón, feria costumes,
all those beautiful women dancing a *Sevillana*...' These words, part
of the farewell press conference given by Julien Escudé, who left
the club six months before Emery arrived, give some idea of the
very special atmosphere in the Andalusian capital, split between two
clubs of almost equal status in terms of supporters, and blessed with
incandescent human warmth.

'I didn't want to leave with some ordinary, banal declaration...
That wouldn't have been a proper description of my life here for
close to six years,' says the French defender, who now runs a meat
restaurant in Madrid with his wife. 'I didn't want to stress Seville as
somewhere where I worked, but as a place I come on holiday to [...]
My farewell was a sort of thank you: thank you for having me, thank
you for those unforgettable years. I'm sometimes asked to describe
Seville in a few words. The first thing that springs to mind is a fiesta.
And in some way, our style of play was a fiesta as well, our spirit was
festive. There was a symbiosis.' Escudé, Dani Alves, Luis Fabiano,
Fernando Navarro and so many others wiped away tears when it
came time to say *adiós,* as if there was a 'before' and 'after' Seville in
their lives. This is even more the case for Coke. Sitting beside Monchi
in the press room, both he and the sporting director burst into tears.
Monchi declared: 'I was wrong. It's not a player who's leaving, it's the

Time to celebrate victory number 1. Benfica defeated on penalties in Europa
League final on 14 May 2014 in Turin.

(Franco Romano/Shutterstock)

The homecoming alongside Sevilla FC's President Jose Castro.

(Epa/Shutterstock)

On the way to collect Europa League trophy number two after victory in Warsaw
against Dnipro.

(Radek Pietruszka/Epa/Shutterstock)

Pure joy.

(Alik Keplicz/AP/Shutterstock)

Alongside Sporting Director 'Monchi' - the man who helped bring in Unai to
change Sevilla's fortunes.

A contrast of emotions. Liverpool, and Jurgen Klopp, defeated in Basel to make it
three Europa League wins in a row for Emery and Sevilla.
(BPI/Shutterstock)

Delivering a speech during celebrations at the Ramon Sanchez-Pizjuan with his
Sevilla team around him.
(Raul Caro/Epa/Shutterstock)

Onto the next challenge. Presentation day at Paris Saint-Germain alongside owner Nasser Al-Khelaifi.

(Christophe Petit Tesson/Epa/Shutterstock)

The job included managing two of the biggest stars in world football in Kylian Mbappé...

(Julien De Rosa/Epa-Efe/Shutterstock)

...and Neymar.

(AP/Shutterstock)

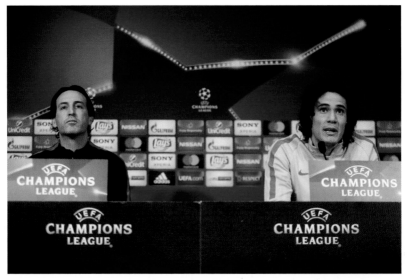

The calm before the storm. Unai alongside another star performer Edinson Cavani
before PSG met Barcelona over two legs in the Champions League in 2016/17.
The first leg ended in a 4-0 win, the second leg a 6-1 defeat.

(AP/Shutterstock)

Meeting the man he would replace - Arsène Wenger.
PSG's meeting with Arsenal in the Champions League in 2016. The game at the
Parc des Princes finished 1-1.

(Kieran McManus/BPI/Shutterstock)

The successor to Wenger. Arsenal's first new leader in 22 years. On tour
in Singapore prior to the start of the 2018/19 season.

(Wallace Woon/Epa-Efe/Shutterstock)

Celebrating the first Premier League win - a 3-1 victory against West Ham United
on 25 August 2018.

(Paul Marriott/Shutterstock)

Unai on the red carpet at The Best FIFA Football Awards in September
2018.

(Facundo Arrizabalaga/Epa-Efe/Shutterstock)

Taking on Europe. One key element of the challenge for Unai at the Emirates.

(Kirsty Wigglesworth/AP/Shutterstock)

heart of the team.' In the room, the sobs of his teammates mingled with the journalists' applause, as they saluted his departure for Schalke 04 after five years of loyal service, first as an extra player, then on the bench with Michel, and finally as vice-captain and the best player in the final against Liverpool, when he scored twice.

'I remember all that and dammit, the tears come into my eyes,' Coke admitted several months later. 'We lived through so much in that dressing room, especially at those bad moments when we all united and went out onto the pitch to fight all together the way the boss wanted... The boss stood up for us, and we did the same. That's how we won glory. And at Seville, when things are going well, *joder*, it's so great. There's a passion for football that you see everywhere. I've had unforgettable nights in that stadium, that city, things I keep in my heart. When you leave, it hurts... It hurts, and even if you take another path, you'll never forget it, and you'll always feel that you're a *Sevillista*.'

A few days after his press conference in the Sánchez-Pizjuán stadium, Coke played his first friendly game for Schalke, against Bologna. He didn't manage to finish even the first half, the rear cruciate ligament in his right knee suddenly giving way: bad luck or a prophecy, who really knows when it's a question of mysterious Seville?

Coke was the symbol of Emery's years at Seville, the dressing room captain. 'He's one of the players who had the greatest influence on my career. I've never known such a kind, helpful guy, someone with no vices who thinks only of the team,' says Abdil Rami. His one weakness seems to have been beer with snails. On the pitch, Coke could fill almost every position, from central midfielder to wing, but above all right-back, where he started out. 'Emery got into the habit of bringing him on towards the end of a game to replace Mariano, the other right-back, or vice-versa. It's rather unusual to change your right-back,' says Clément Loubière, a freelance French journalist based in Andalusia who is an attentive spectator from the press box. There's even a scarf you can buy that reads *Coke por Mariano* and a song as well! In European games, Emery used them both, with Coke playing in front of Mariano. 'That was a more defensive choice, which some fans criticised Emery for during his last season. Perhaps it's our character, our way of looking at life, but Seville expects a show,' according to Carlos Romero, a historian who is the author of the excellent *Mentiras del Fútbol Sevillano* [*Lies about Football in Seville*]. One only has to look at the stands to see the truth of this: some people are laughing, others smiling, several generations of the same family, and elegantly dressed young men everywhere. In Seville, people go to the football as though they're going to the theatre or a bullfight; it just depends on the poster. And in the midst of the crowd, the young women of Seville... in evening wear, with red dresses and white jackets, occasionally a rose in their hair. Their eyes shine with a light that women from the north will never have: at least according to Théophile Gautier.

The Andalusian capital has inspired many artists and writers, some of them born there, like Diego Vélasquez and Antonio Machado, others who have merely visited over the centuries: Miguel de Cervantes, Tirso de Molina, Prosper Mérimée or Unai Emery, the most recent in modern-day history. From the touchline, he traces his work with fingers, hands, his head, sometimes even his hips. An abstract art that's as visual as it is vocal when he tells a defensive midfielder to push forward before turning to face the public, slightly circumspect, as if in a painting by Pablo Picasso.[22] 'If one was being true to life, you couldn't paint a hundred pictures with the same subject,' the artist from Málaga used to repeat. Of course, he couldn't have suspected that his concept would be applied to football. 'I've played in different positions for Unai, as in the return match against Betis in the Europa League. I hadn't played for a while, but he said I

---

22 This conjures up an image of a decision taken regularly by Emery to move Vicente Iborra. 'This was one of the tactical changes that wasn't very well received at first, because no one understood it. Iborra was the number ten or second striker, he was more of a finisher. His position further up the field allowed Banega to come back and operate lower down the pitch where he wasn't marked. If we were under pressure, Ever was there, and Iborra dropped back to play as a defensive midfielder,' explains Juan Carlos Carcedo. Rami adds: 'When Barça were pressing us hard, Unai brought Iborra back. Whenever the goalkeeper couldn't pass the ball out without a problem, he would lob it to Iborra (1 metre 95 in height). 'If we win the ball, we send it to Gameiro one-on-one. If we lose it, we go for the second ball. They're really strong on the ground, but we can thrash them in an aerial duel!'

was to be a central midfielder: "I've got more confidence in you than you have in yourself. I know you're going to play well." Following that conversation, it's true that I began to have more self-belief, and I wasn't the only one who felt that way,' says Coke, referring to all the young players and others not necessarily known to the public who came to replace the ones who left each summer: Rakitic and Vidal to Barcelona, Bacca to Milan, or Alberto Moreno to Liverpool. 'The first months after my arrival, I didn't play much, which was normal, it took time to adjust to a new championship, a fresh demand,' says Timothée Kolodziejczak, brought in from Nice in 2014. 'Unai always told me not to worry, to work hard, because he was going to use me and give me a role over the season. That's what was so good: he managed to make me feel involved even when I was on the bench. And he kept his word, because by the end of my first season I was in the starting eleven.'

Obviously, the successes in the Europa League managed to hide some of the shortcomings of the Emery era, such as an inability to win away from home, notably in his last year in the *Liga*, where the record is catastrophic: 9 draws, 9 losses, and no wins! Nor did he ever manage to get the most out of some talented soloists, such as Ciro Immobile or Yevhen Konoplyanka, two players he had not wanted – he didn't speak to Monchi for several weeks because of that, endlessly repeating that they should have recruited Raphaël Guerreiro from Lorient. It was the same story with Gerard Deulofeu, lent for a season by Barça, without success.

'I remember seeing Unai give Deulofeu a real shock before he sent him on the field from the bench during one match. His handshake was shall we say quite robust,' laughs Clément Loubière. A very Basque way of treating people, which nobody ever managed to avoid, not even Unai's "adopted sons", Rami and Vitolo. 'In the dressing room, they kept on saying he was my father, but I was treated exactly the same as the others if I didn't play well,' says Vitolo with a laugh, a constant first choice for the club and then for the national side.

This description of Emery as a father was taken even more seriously by one player, whom everyone considered as 'extra-sensitive': Ever Banega. 'What's the first thing I think of regarding

Unai? That's easy, he's like a father to me.' This is a phrase sometimes used by young footballers to describe their relationship with a person who has brought them on, but rarely of their manager when they're adult. 'I've learnt so much from him... he changed the way I play. I learnt to press in different ways, to manage pressure, to get closer to the goal – something he often repeated to me – but above all always to help my teammates in any way possible. I've never been an individualist, but I didn't work so hard for the team in the past. And I've learnt on a human level as well. Above all on that level, I think...'

And yet, at first the relationship between the two men was far from easy. In Emery's second season at Valencia, Banega came back from a loan to Atlético Madrid (24 games in *La Liga*), without any guarantee that he would be part of the manager's rotation. 'We had very strong arguments at the time,' the Argentine international confirms. He is a player described by Mikel Jauregi as 'someone a bit different, in his own world, capable of incredible kindness and sensitivity, but harder to manage than others as well.'

This portrait is confirmed by the players of the time, Rami above all: 'Most coaches say: "I'm the boss, I do as I want!" But not Unai. He succeeded in adapting to Banega's character, which was unheard of. Ever didn't run that much at the beginning, but gradually he made more effort for everyone because he's a guy who gives. The coach knew he could be an enormous bonus in attack with the great technique he has, so he adapted to him, although he never renounced his principles. He put him on the same wavelength as us.'

Of course, the two men quarrelled a lot, to such an extent that Sofiane Feghouli pointed out that: 'Unai really doesn't bear a grudge, if he brought him to Seville!' Banega was brought in during the summer of 2014 with the same number as Rakitic, who had left for Barcelona. 'While he was waiting for the two clubs to sign the agreement, he trained on his own. My brother sent him texts asking how he was, and to go easy on the McDonalds,' says Igor with a laugh.

At Seville, Banega came into his own as a midfield-playmaker, at first behind Carlos Bacca, then Kevin Gameiro, another player with whom Unai had a stormy relationship. The Frenchman is naturally timid and says little, but he works hard on the drills his manager demands: pressing, different calls and throw-ins. 'The Europa League quarter-final at home. A penalty shoot-out against Bilbao. Kevin had cramp and could barely walk. Unai looked at him and said: "You can take the fifth penalty, the one that's going to win us qualification." He had complete confidence in him as a finisher, especially with penalties. And that's what happened: his shot went straight into the net,' recalls Kolodziejczak.

With 29 goals in all competitions in his last season at Seville, every weekend Gameiro stirred the passion of the BNs, the *Biris Norte*, the group of ultra fans clustered behind the northern goal. 'They often chanted *Ga-mé-ro*, he was enormously popular among the fans,' Loubière confirms. With Emery as well, who was constantly promising him during their private discussions: 'you'll be in the French team in a few months.'

This promise was kept, as was another one made over a cup of coffee at Banega's house in February 2016. 'He went home one afternoon. Unai had signed a contract for him to go to Inter Milan that summer and wanted to be sure his mind was still with Seville. They spoke together for hours, and both swore that they'd give all they could to win another Europa League championship', Igor recalls. And so, when Banega came in angry and disappointed at half-time in the second leg of the semi-final against Shakhtar, Emery took the lead. 'We conceded a goal right at the end of the half, to make it 1-1. Ever was down, so I took him into my office. We talked for several minutes, man-to-man. I told him we needed him, that he was the beacon for the team.' While he was doing this, Juan Carlos Carcedo was taking care of the other players in the dressing room, without this causing any problem, according to Coke. 'The boss was very fond of Banega, and he felt the same way. He treated him like his son: he got annoyed with him as you do with a child. Occasionally in training they really tore into each other, but they always made it up afterwards.'

Rumour in the corridors had it that when things weren't going well the Argentine player would hide in the toilets, the showers, or simply in the dressing room so as not to show his tears. 'Yes, there were tears, of course there were!' Banega admits. 'When I saw he was right in our arguments… He helped me become a better man, a better player. Even today I don't know how to thank him enough for all that, for his patience, for the fact that he understood me.'

As a thank you, the attacking midfielder in fact 'did things on the pitch that you don't see with other players. He was Seville's playmaker, the one who controlled the tempo of the game. He was the one who gave the game a structure,' says Coke admiringly, adding that 'Ever's generosity is something that only his teammates are aware of.'

Irresistible in the second half against Shakhtar (3-1 at the final whistle), the Argentine star led his colleagues to the final against Liverpool – a match during which he was surprisingly ordinary. Played in Basle, the Reds dominated the first half of the game, going in at the break 1-0 up thanks to a goal from Sturridge. 'I was thinking: how can you encourage the team? How can you motivate them? I remembered where we were the strongest, where we felt most loved, the most supported, and so I said to them: "Imagine that we're in the Sánchez-Pizjuán stadium, with our public, at home in Seville!"' Unai recalls. It was a very powerful speech, according to Coke. 'They were playing a lot better than us, then came half-time. The boss asked us to imagine we were playing at home, where we always won. I don't know how, but the whole team seemed to believe it. Then he outlined several small tactical things, especially one move that we did immediately at the start of the second half, and which brought our equaliser. That second half was a demonstration of our style of play. We had only created one chance before the break, but Unai freed us all, as if we had no responsibilities, had nothing to lose.'

To always have self-belief, even in the darkest moments and the final minutes: that was without doubt the real transformation of Seville under Emery. 'During our training sessions, he kept on telling us to go flat out right to the last minute. When we were nearing the end, he would demand an extra effort: "Imagine we're losing 1-2 and it's the last action in the game, when you have to give your all…" All those goals in the last few minutes weren't a coincidence,' adds the Spaniard, who did not though raise the Copa del Rey four days later, when Seville were beaten 0-2 by Barcelona after extra-time.

Following this game, the last time Emery was to manage the *Nervionenses*, the players and their families stayed on at a Madrid hotel to celebrate the club's success in the Europa League, and the season as a whole. A glass of beer in hand, Ever Banega also knew he had played his last match for the club. Discreetly, he went up to Igor and whispered in his ear: 'You have to persuade your brother to come to Inter Milan with me…'

15.2

INTERVIEW WITH ADIL RAMI

Adil Rami knew Unai at Valencia and Seville. His teammates liked to tease him, saying that the manager 'is in fact your father'… a joke the Frenchman is happy to accept, as someone who himself tries to keep all the different groups in the dressing room happy. On the pitch, he made himself one of Emery's stalwarts, playing 53 and then 46 games in all competitions during their last two seasons together.

First impressions

'He surprised me from the start, but not necessarily because of his gifts as a trainer. When I arrived I couldn't speak Spanish, and he really helped me and my family to acclimatise. Some coaches promise to do that, but it's all talk, they don't really care. That wasn't the case with Unai: he really cared about every player and liked to converse with them to get to know one another as human beings.'

Daily management

'I've been a professional for ten years now, and I've learned a few things. One of them is that a trainer can really change a player. That's what happened with me under Unai. He knew how active I was, and so he often used to advise me: "You're a force of nature. In a tackle, you're going to win a lot of them, but sometimes there'll be fouls because you're pretty strong, so you have to stay calm." As far as restarts are concerned, he wanted to try different things. He doesn't want you to mess around, for you to lack respect, but if you lose the ball in restarting an attack, he won't say anything, because in a way that's his responsibility. When a manager tells you that, you're cool. He doesn't shout at you like lots of others do: "Shit, you should control the ball and pass it, but not a long ball up the pitch!" The only time Unai shouts at you is if you don't run, if you don't make any effort for the team. If you get a pass or a control of the ball wrong, he doesn't linger over that, but on your reaction and how you're going to deal with it… Sincerely, that changes a player completely, it's astounding.'

How do you manage a player who is too active?

'After I'd been at Valencia for a while, Unai called me in after a session and asked me to stop training the way I was doing, to stop always going at it full tilt. That's rare [laughs]. According to him, I was too energetic: "I don't want you to run all over the place, right and left all the time. If we can't keep up behind you, you're causing problems for the team." He told me that when he saw I'd understood he liked guys who gave their all. Afterwards, he called me in I don't know how often to get me to calm down: "I don't want you to run so much, to go looking for tackles so often …" and so on. I've always needed to channel my energy. Even when I'm on holiday, if I don't get my daily dose of sport or feel really fatigued, I feel like shit, because I'm on the border of being hyperactive. So yeah, Unai sometimes used to hold his head in his hands because I did scissor kicks when we worked on set pieces in training [laughs]. All I wanted to do was score, and he couldn't blame me for that because he shouted at me for only scoring three goals the previous season: "That's crap, Adil, crap! It's not good enough!"'

Tactical work

'Every week, he starts with a video showing what our objectives are. And this is different every week. For example: "We have a very high line, and we're open to counter-attacks. So, we're going to work on covering back." He wants to work with the guy who's at the back, all on his own, who has to cover everything. What's most important is not the player who goes to tackle their attacker, because he can slip, or can be dribbled around. What matters is the player who has to cover and regain the ball. So Unai would show us videos about that, and then we'd train, concentrating on that aspect. In one exercise, the midfielders were overrun, so we had to drop back a little, not too far, to slow the opposing attacker down and allow our midfield to get back and recover the ball.

'Everything is calculated, he talks about every metre, every centimetre. The next day, a guy is in front of me, and unluckily it's Lionel Messi, and he's sure to dribble past me. In the video, Unai looks at everything around me: "Why is Messi in a one-on-one with Rami? Where's my number six? Why do you let Messi do that? Why don't you help Rami? His vision is always collective. That reminds me of a goal I scored from a free-kick, something we'd practised for hours. We often had a screen to leave me free or the opposite. Well, in the video, Carcedo was full of praise for the other players, but didn't mention me: "Congratulations, it's thanks to you lot that we scored!" And what about me, for god's sake? [*laughs*].'

Talks in the dressing room

'His talks are great, and they're different every day. I'm a bit more mature these days, but I used to have to take a deep breath, because his talks were so good that when I left the dressing room I wanted to tear into the opposition. He could motivate the team, but I was already motivated enough without the talk... Sometimes even, I'd try not to listen. It's like Obelix, the cartoon character, I didn't need to drink the magic portion because I fell in a cauldron of it when I was little [*laughs*]. For example, I remember a derby against Betis. He knew I could lose it and I needed his help: "Shit, stop getting into trouble, stop doing this, stop doing that!" He really went for me at half-time! I took his criticism because I was a bit more mature than before, but I had to lock myself in the toilet because it looked as if everything was going down the drain. In the second half, I played steadily, and didn't have any clashes with the opposing side. That's when you know you've got a really good manager.

'Unai knew I could blow a fuse, get booked and damage our team. He'd seen that, he knew it was coming, and so he shouted at me so that all the drama would be in the dressing room. When I went back out onto the pitch I played well, and I was even man of the match according to the press, but he couldn't give a damn about that [*laughs*].'

The best moment with Unai Emery

'The final against Liverpool, no doubt about it. First there was his half-time talk, when he was so calm: "Don't panic lads. Keep on pressing, keep on attacking. They're bound to crack!" I felt he had managed to calm all of us down. Then after the final whistle, I hugged him and thanked him a thousand times. I wasn't all over him, I was just so grateful. People can say what they like, that he's my old man or whatever, but they don't know Unai. He'll be the first to shout at me and leave me on the bench if that's what I deserve. If I play again for a manager like that and he leaves me on the bench for every match, that simply means I don't deserve to play. And if I do, I'll be in the starting eleven. [...]

'When I was going through a bad patch in my footballing career, my mum would say that I needed to work with Unai again because our characters are compatible. I was on holiday in Dubai with my wife and he called me: "Come with me! You'll play, you'll get back to your best, score goals, get back into the French team, and play in the European Championships." It was only a two minute-call, straight to the point, no messing. Today I hear my name Adil Rami chanted in the Sánchez-Pizjuán stadium, the one with the best atmosphere in all Spain, I think. Before I got that call from Unai, I really couldn't have imagined that. No big club wanted me. It's also thanks to the new manager at Seville, for whom I have a very soft spot, but everything that's happened to me, the French national team, the European Championships, is thanks to Unai. The same goes for my twins, who are Seville born and bred thanks to him! [*laughs*].'

16

LIVING ON A VOLCANO

Michael Calvin is one of the most famous writers in the literature of football. A former *Daily Telegraph* sports editor, in recent years he has received many awards, above all in 2014 for his book *The Nowhere Men*, about the life of club scouts. Unlike many others who stick to a certain style or area, Calvin explores new perspectives with each book. On 13 August 2015, his latest work appeared. It had a particularly appropriate title: *Living on the Volcano: The Secrets of Surviving as a Football Manager*. On the cover was a photo of Arsène Wenger, crouching down, head in hands. The angle of the shot, from behind the Arsenal manager, suggested that a manager can be overwhelmed by the crowd, the state of the game, or the pressure inherent to the job of manager. 'There are many factors for measuring success, but the key ingredients will always be the passion the individual has for the sport; his skill at evolving and adapting, and of course, an eye for talent,' Wenger wrote in his preface to the book.

Passion, psychology, evolution, adaptation and instinct: everything Unai Emery has cleverly amassed in his managerial career. 'He's the complete manager, who gives you everything so that you can succeed,' in the view of Sofiane Feghouli. 'Athletically and physically, you'll be on top form: thanks to him, I greatly increased my involvement in each game. Tactically, he prepares you the whole week for the match, you know exactly how to hurt the opposition and in which phase of the game. Mentally, he lets you play your game, and psychologically, he stirs you up so much in the pre-match talk that you want to take a bite out of your opponent's leg! Individually, collectively, everything is ready. All you have to do is play: and so, if things go wrong, it's your responsibility.'

The Algerian international knows how much he owes to Emery, a manager who tried to persuade him to come to Seville. 'It's true, we had some arguments,' says the player with a smile, but he appreciates Emery's style of man management: 'You might not like the way he looks, and he might not like you, but that will never get in the way of his choices. There were several occasions at Valencia when it wasn't always easy [*laughs*]. In one training session, one of the players wanted to punch Unai. He just looked at him quietly, not bothered. We calmed the player down, because it could have become a real fight. The important thing is that Unai didn't take that into account if he needed him for a particular role in a match. I think they had it out, and Unai gave him another chance. Adil Rami is right, he's a gentleman. that's why the players respect him. He doesn't do things behind your back, it's always up front.'

Feghouli's next encounter with Unai had to be postponed, for a while at least. At the end of May 2016, the temporary sporting director at PSG, Olivier Létang, got in touch with the Basque manager. Another European suitor, after Everton and Milan, who had been trying to woo him for two years, with Adriano Galliani calling him on several occasions. 'In 2015, West Ham had made him an offer. It was a close call, but he decided to stay with Seville. Napoli were interested as well. His lawyer went to see them, but after his experience at Spartak, Unai preferred to say no, because there were no guarantees of a stable project,' explains Igor.

The project at PSG was of a different order, since the club had the ambition of catching up with the best European clubs, although not necessarily of winning the Champions League in the short term. This was what the club president Nasser Al-Khelaïfi, who personally took charge of the negotiations, repeatedly told Emery. A meeting was arranged in Valencia between Nasser, Olivier Létang and Unai. 'I asked Nasser: "Why do you want to sign me? What are you looking for from me?" Emery told Diego Torres, an *El País* journalist. "He replied: because you're on an upward path, you've won three consecutive Europa Leagues. It's not the same as the Champions League, but to do that with a team like Seville is very difficult. You have a winner's genes. And we're a team accustomed to winning but which has to improve certain details."'

In short, he wanted PSG to begin a new era, with a method different from that of Laurent Blanc; not necessarily better or worse, simply different. After a lightning visit to Doha, where he met an old acquaintance, Roberto Olabe – then head of the Aspire sporting academy before his return to Real Sociedad – Unai signed a two-year contract, with an option for a third. All that was left was to reach an agreement between PSG, Seville and Emery, whose contract there ended in 2017.

Apparently nothing more than a trifle, in the end this took several weeks, due to a petty quarrel over a bonus for qualification for the Champions League.

The bosses at Seville claimed this should only be paid if the club qualified because of its position in *La Liga*, rather than success in the Europa League. A laughable sideshow for a club still massively affected by the departure of Monchi, a painful separation resolved at a meeting of the board on 30 May 2016, only 12 days after the triumph against Liverpool.

The sporting director was used to this kind of thing, confessing every year how 'fed up' he was by the fact that 'the character Monchi' had become more important than the real Ramón Rodríguez Verdejo. In fact, he had signed a contract with Almería to escape from this 'monster' and to protect his family. 'My wife was depressed and we needed to get out of Seville,' he told the journalist Alvaro Corazon Rural. What happened next is told by Roberto Arrocha, the co-author of Monchi's biography and presenter of a programme on the club's

TV channel. 'It was a difficult decision, especially since the club had won the UEFA Cup [now the Europa League] thanks to that famous goal by Antonio Puerta in the semi-final against Schalke.[23] It was during Seville's *feria*, and that game changed everything. Monchi went to see the club's president José Maria del Nido and told him: 'I can't leave. I can't ignore the feelings I have deep down.' He got in his car and drove to Almería to meet the club president, Alfonso Garcia. He explained that he wouldn't be joining the club but promised to help him whenever he could. Apparently, before leaving, he gazed at Garcia and said: "I can't live without my team..."

Apart from the fact that he would have been able to work sooner with Emery, this visceral attachment to Seville has been the chief concern of his entourage, as for example when in spring 2015 there were approaches from Manchester United and... PSG. 'A defeat leaves him broken-hearted. To see his Seville beaten really hurts him,' say several long-time employees at the club. The pressure was sometimes overwhelming, to such an extent that sometimes Monchi burst into tears when people weren't looking, and occasionally in front of everyone, as during a meeting with the club's top officials where he admitted he couldn't bear it any longer. After that, he took refuge in silence and isolation, never leaving home or his office. His only concerns at that time? To go to the workout room every day from 7 a.m. to 9 a.m. and to work, more and more...

After a couple of month's respite, when he wouldn't take anyone's calls, especially from the soon-to-depart Emery, he began again, organizing a new era at Seville with the arrival of the Argentine trainer Jorge Sampaoli.

At the same time, Unai was presented to the press as the new coach of PSG on 28 June 2016, without having left the Andalusian capital as he would have wished. The move caused a regrettable misunderstanding, fortunately now settled, between Monchi and

---

23 Antonio Puerta's goal in extra-time qualified Seville for its first European final. It remains a striking symbol of this child of the club, who died tragically on 28 August 2007, at the age of 22, after suffering a heart attack during a game against Getafe.

Emery, who had been friends for three and a half years – their relationship going beyond the merely professional. Curiously, even if everything appears to set Andalusians against Basques (whose clichés have been crudely exposed in the 'comedy' *Ocho Apellidos Vascos* [*Eight Basque Names*], the two men are in fact very similar: hard-working, passionate, talkative, and above all, stubborn…

Unai's departure couldn't though conceal what was the essential for him: to manage one of the greatest clubs in the world. A further evolution in his career. 'It's a different culture. Football isn't seen or played in the same way in the Basque country, Seville, Moscow or Paris,' he says. His brother Igor adds: 'He's changing because he has to adapt, to keep up-to-date. He is faced with new situations, and that enriches him. In Paris he realised that he had to approach the training sessions more calmly, and that was new for him.'

In fact, some PSG players reacted badly to Emery's methods, especially when he greatly increased the intensity of the training and video sessions: although after consulting the squad, these were reduced in the autumn. 'We knew what we did badly in Moscow, and we weren't going to make the same mistakes in Paris,' says Juan Carlos Carcedo. He insisted their management style was more flexible, that they listened more to the players, and could speak the language better.

'That was the first thing I told him when he signed: learn French quickly, make sure you're comfortable in the language. Your strong point is what you communicate to each player, to the group, so you need to speak French,' recalls Manuel Llorente, his former president at Valencia.

Unlike with Russian, Emery made rapid progress in French, helped by a teacher and by his brother, who lived with him half the year in Paris. 'I've been working full-time for Unai for a year and a half,' Igor said in 2016. 'I created his internet site in 2010, and since then I've taken care of the communication side of things, relations with the press, and many other things that are between the two of us.'

Little things like the famous letter to the PSG supporters, posted on Unai's site on 13 November 2016 and mocked by *L'Equipe* a few days later in a front-page article on the manager's 'over-communication'. 'We've been doing that since Valencia,' says his brother. We did it at Seville and Spartak, where it was even translated into Russian. As far as that particular letter is concerned, they were Unai's words, but corrected by me because he didn't yet have the knowledge to write properly in French. He doesn't need me in Spanish, but he does in French.'

This anecdote illustrates the media frenzy that surrounded Unai when he went to PSG. Most of it attacking him: one journalist calling him a 'marmoset' live on I'Télé, another describing as a 'pyromaniac in *France Football* and a third ridiculing him as a coach who trained the team 'like an eight-year-old child' in *Le Parisien*.

'They ran him down all the time, but he has won more awards than the whole of French football. It's incredible, isn't it? You have to know nothing about football to come out with things like that,' says Rami, backed up by all the people I've spoken to, including critics like Dmitri Popov. 'Why wouldn't he be able to manage a big club like PSG? What happened at Spartak was years ago, and even despite that I've never doubted that he could coach a top team. He's among the very best.'

Emery came up against what a number of his non-French predecessors had faced while working in *Ligue 1*, especially Leonardo Jardim and Marcelo Bielsa, a coach 'who has influenced him' and with whom in the early days he used to have a coffee and talk about football. 'I've worked with both of them and can understand the similarities, because both of them have a love of communicating about their profession,' says Nicolas Faure, occasional interpreter for Emery at press conferences, just as he had been for Marcelo Bielsa in his last weeks at Marseille. 'But they're very different all the same. Bielsa never relaxes, there's a bearish side to him, whereas Unai knows how to take things, to be more sociable. He's more interested in the people around him.'

Admired by all the great managers, Bielsa was vilified by the French media circus, apart from some notable exceptions (Daniel Riolo, Didier Roustan, Omar Da Fonseca or Luis Fernández, among the best known.) Worst of all, his resignation from Marseille after the first game of the 2015-16 season against Caen, led to him being reduced to the ranks of a 'mercenary' or 'louse'.

This is a reaction that drives Faure wild. 'It's shows an incredible lack of respect. I've seen extraordinary things from the inside, especially regarding that last match. Shortly before the final whistle, his assistant, Diego Reyes, told me to go to Bielsa's office after the game. I thought he mustn't have been happy with some translations. When I went in, they were both at the computer, busy analysing the match. Bielsa handed me a letter and asked me to translate it word for word. At the same time, he was talking about Thauvin's performance and how it could be improved, and I can't remember what else. I quickly skimmed the letter and suddenly saw the word "resignation". I looked up, and Bielsa told me to read it a second time. I did so, but I said to myself "it's not possible, he's busy talking about next week's training with his assistant." He had penned his resignation before the match, but there he was studying the aspects of collective and individual progress of every player after that same match! It was so crazy I thought I was dreaming. He asked me to read the letter again for a third time, this time following his finger word for word, to make sure he would be correctly understood [...] At the end of the post-match press conference, when he had answered all the questions, he signalled to me to read the letter. Of course, it was an astonishing moment, almost beyond belief. But what I remember about him is above all his kindness and the fact that he lived for football. He's a genius, with all the good qualities and defects that entails.'

Bielsa is neither an angel nor a devil, but such a strong personality that he divides opinion: either you worship him, even when he's heading straight for a brick wall, or you loathe him and accuse him of chasing after money from the Mexican national team – a position that in the end he never took up.

Without going to these extremes, Emery suffers from the same problem. Some people call him a genius at the slightest change he makes, a description neither he nor his friends approve of. For example, Mikel Jauregi said, 'He's not the greatest manager on earth, if such a thing exists, but there's no doubt he's the one who works the hardest'. And on the other hand, the majority of the media protests in Paris about his 'arrogance', his 'air of wanting to teach us lessons', or of 'ruining Ben Arfa's talent', as *Le Figaro* wrote, without bothering to add the criticisms that several top officials made of the player: 'What exactly have you won in your career?'; 'Brother, you're just scratching your balls!'; "We'll buy you a ball, that'll be better![24]

In the same way, some TV director or sports news editors asked their journalists to find people 'willing to go on camera to say Emery isn't up to managing star players,' without even having heard those players' opinions!

This kind of attack makes little sense, especially if one takes into account what the stars in question, for example: David Villa, David Silva, Jordi Alba and Juan Mata, four *fuoriclasse* whose talent really isn't any less than that of the current PSG players; a glance at all the awards they've won puts an end to any such debate. 'He's a great manager, and above all a great person,' according to David Villa, European and World champion with Spain, three times champion of *La Liga* and the Copa del Rey, and also a winner of the Champions League, a European Supercup and the World Club Championship with Barça. 'He helped me a lot, and obviously I made progress with him. I was a finisher, but he wanted me to combine with the wingers as well, to change positions with them from time to time, to go out wide to stretch the defence.'

These tactical choices were often debated within the squad, sometimes vehemently on both sides. 'Of course, that happened, of course! I think that what's good in football is precisely to talk and argue, because that way you learn and progress more. Unai enjoys that kind of discussion, and he's right, it's better for the team,' adds

---

24 Many PSG players didn't want to play alongside Ben Arfa in the first months after his arrival in the French capital. But the player listened to his colleagues' complaints about his selfishness (and his physical condition) and worked on correcting his mistakes – an attitude that impressed everyone inside the club.

Villa. He ends by comparing Unai with all the other great managers he has known in his career (Luis Aragonés, Vincente Del Bosque, Pep Guardiola, Diego Simeone, etc.): 'They all have a lot in common, but I've always liked Unai's way of working. His way of always wanting to improve, and of analysing every opponent point by point in order to offer his players as much information as possible. Honestly, it was a great experience in my career to share two seasons with him like that.'

Strong words from a player who wasn't particularly close to Unai, unlike Mata or Silva. And yet for most Parisian football fans, Emery wasn't a name to conjure with, not a manager who could help PSG progress. The Europa League isn't the Champions League, Seville isn't Paris Saint-Germain, went the arguments time and again, even though Sergio Rico, Escudero, Mariano, Coke, Banega, Vitolo or Krohn-Dehli (before his injury) could outclass almost all the other players in their positions in *Ligue 1*.

'We discovered things were done differently in France. They placed less emphasis on analysis and comprehension of the game. Then there was transparency: that seemed to be unknown here. Journalists rang me to speak on behalf of my brother or for me to tell them who was in the team, to give them info,' complains Igor, often shocked by the nature of the calls.

'It was following the press conference when Unai used some bottles of water to demonstrate a point, as he had done in Seville. A journalist from *L'Équipe* called me that evening: "Was that deliberate, intentional? Was it to create a buzz, to sell more, to make people laugh?" At first, I thought he was joking *(laughs)*. Unai was limited in French, and so he tried to get his message across by means of gestures. If there had been two stones on the table, he would have used them. He wanted to talk about competition, about the way he manages a dressing room. It was spontaneous, not pre-meditated. That may, in fact, be his problem: he really thinks everyone is honest.'

At the weekend, for fun, Unai would ask him 'what have they written about me this week that's nice,' not that he took the media barrage that seriously. 'As far as his choices or his work are concerned, it doesn't have the slightest influence. But he also knows it can have consequences, especially in increasing the pressure when there are poor results, and possibly the risk of getting him sacked. The players can feel this pressure as well, and some of them aren't strong enough to cope, and that can lead to a drop in performance.'

With pressure from the media or not, Emery continued serenely on his way, with the ambition of winning the Champions League. Not necessarily in his first season – the bosses at PSG were not utopian – but one day. To achieve that, he 'would have to suffer, as all managers do [...] Anyone who doesn't, isn't really a manager,' Igor concluded. There would be a learning process, a questioning of himself, a more united dressing room and discussions with his leaders, above all

Marco Verratti, who always wants to give his point of view, whether or not he agrees with the coach.

'We like it when the players come to talk to us, to explain what they think. It's a reaction, a sign of an interest in the group,' according to Carcedo. Obviously, his and Emery's future depend on the results of every club they work at. 'At PSG, there were some mistakes, some moments of doubt, even of misunderstanding, as when Unai mimed putting a pistol against the temple of a player who didn't understand his instructions. He had already made the same gesture back in Valencia to get his message across, an action that brought laughter. In Paris, however, some people saw this as another act of folly from a manager occasionally donning the mantle of the professor, the *maestro* forcing his students to come to the front and address the class. This is a method used by others, Guardiola the first among them, but not necessarily accepted in France, a football world closed in on itself and its certainties, lacking any desire to be open to others; a conception to which Emery will never adhere.' Unai has many faults – who hasn't? – but not that one. 'We were talking recently and he asked me if I was up to speed on the techniques adopted by a particular manager in *Segunda B*', recalls Alberto Benito, a *Madrileño* he met more than 20 years earlier at Toledo. 'When I was a sporting director in Cyprus, he wanted information about the way people work there, because he thought he could learn something. Even though he's at PSG, he always wants to learn.'

One never finishes learning, especially in the Champions League. When the greatest clubs in the world came to the Parc des Princes, Unai would, as usual, write some quotes on the whiteboard for his pre-match talk. Taken from the books he read, one of them would perhaps simply repeat the words used by a manager one autumn evening at the Seville training centre: 'He who learns travels far.'

17.1

TO DESCEND INTO HELL, THEN CLIMB OUT

More than a year after the publication of *El Maestro* in France, PSG knew how things stood. Their coach even more so. 'Something always happens when you're a manager,' says Unai with a smile. 'You can never be relaxed…' He sighs, then goes on: 'I never doubted the group or the direction we were going in. Never.'

The reference to their sensational elimination from the Champions League by Barcelona in March 2017 is implicit, as is the loss of the championship to Monaco two months later after four years of undisputed reign. The 87 points won (the third highest total in the club's history)[25] and success in the Champions Trophy, the League Cup and the French Cup weren't enough. After all, PSG hadn't sacked Laurent Blanc and signed a new manager only to win national trophies. 'It was a season… you could call foundational. We did good things on the pitch, we won lots of points in the French championship as in other years, but that wasn't enough,' says Edinson Cavani, one of those who profited the most from Emery's arrival. 'The coach and I share the same passion for football, and the same desire to improve. I don't always agree with him, but that's normal, players never completely agree with their trainer (*laughs*). He gave me

---

25 Monaco won the second highest number of points in the history of *Ligue 1*, amassing 95. PSG holds the record, with 96 points in the 2015-16 season.

responsibility and put his trust in me, so I tried to pay him back on the pitch.'

Voted best player in the French championship, the Uruguayan did more than repay Unai's trust. And yet for him the start of the season had been difficult. In the second match against Metz, he missed absolutely everything in front of goal, to the exasperation of the fans in the Parc des Princes. The same thing happened in the first game of the Champions League against Arsenal, despite scoring the first goal. Doubts about him were building up. 'The next day, we discussed it. 'I admitted that I had several clear chances,' said Cavani. 'Emery reassured me, saying, "The most important thing for me is that you create chances. I'm happy if you do that, but we have to work hard to be more effective, to turn those chances into goals".

That discussion was decisive, according to Edinson's adviser and half-brother, Walter Guglielmone. 'He showed great faith in him when a lot of people thought his shoulders weren't broad enough to replace Zlatan. That day Unai even told Edi he was wrong, that he wasn't going to score 35 goals that season, but 50! He told him he was more than capable of it. We looked at one another, we both thought he was crazy! (laughs). But no, he really thought that and wanted to push Edi to go beyond his limits.' Three days later at Caen, Cavani left the pitch at half-time after scoring four goals. By the end of the season, he scored 49 goals in 50 games in all competitions, the best total since the start of his career.

The Matador's success was one of Emery's achievements in his first season, as was the incorporation of the young Presnel Kimpembe in defence, imperious at home against Barcelona. Also noteworthy was the regular use of Adrien Rabiot as a sweeper – a position where Laurent Blanc had tried him as well – but none of that can help erase the memory of 'that damn match' in the Camp Nou, to repeat the remark made by Romain Grunstein, the head kit manager for the team. 'In three months we saw everything. After the 4-0 victory at home, it was as if we'd won the World Cup. I've never known such euphoria.'

That victory, one of the most brilliant of PSG's history in Europe, was a collective effort, in attack and in defence. 'We wanted to stop Busquets releasing the ball,' explains Unai. 'So we asked Cavani to stick close to him, then later to cover Piqué, because their team adapted as the match went on. He had to do both things, still watching out for Busquets.' The objective was summed up simply by his assistant, Juan Carlos Carcedo: 'To prevent Barça from playing fluidly, to push them to try to do something else.'

It was a mission fully accomplished for the Basque trainer, who, however, went back into the dressing room looking slightly worried. 'We have our own room, with lots of photos on the walls. I wanted one with the coach, and thought it was a good moment', Romain Grunstein recalls. Unai said: "No problem, but when we've qualified." I replied that we had won 4-0, but he brought me down to earth immediately: "Yes, we're leading 4-0, but we haven't won anything. The danger is to believe we've won."'

Despite the draw against Toulouse five days later, Paris was wild with excitement. Club officials were already looking up hotels in Cardiff, the host city for the final, to find rooms for the team and followers. 'We crushed Marseille soon afterwards (5-1), so we got the impression it seemed only logical that the 4-0 was the start of something,' says Romain, who at the time could see the staff were uneasy. 'Unai never stopped repeating that the return match was still to come. He said once: "Do you really believe Barcelona will just wait for us, or that they want to get their revenge? We have to be ready for the fight, to be confident but prepared."'

At the same time, the French press, especially *L'Equipe*, spread the idea of a *remontada*, which translates as 'recovery', a word used ad nauseam in the days leading up to the match on 8 March 2017. Morning, noon and night, the viewers of *L'Equipe 21* and other news channels, sports broadcasters or not, were constantly reminded of the possibility of a historic comeback. The same message was to be found on the internet and in the newspapers, which the players obviously read on their smartphones. Worse still, Bros. Stories, an internet site supposedly showing athletes in a different light, for once had a disastrous idea: to bring together Meunier, Matuidi, Verratti and Draxler in a pizzeria to discuss a single topic: 'How do you really feel about the return match?' As if Barcelona were in need of motivation, the PSG players gave them even more encouragement, just in case.

'The social media in the dressing room was harmful during the preparation for the match. But it had become a way of integrating for the group. You take photos, make short videos, some of them were really hooked', say some of the staff. All that exasperated Juan Carlos Carcedo, who advised some of the players: 'Discretion and simplicity are just as good.'

By playing the match before even stepping out onto the pitch, the whole club was making a mistake. To make things worse, the squad was decimated. Thiago Motta still had the injured calf that had prevented him playing in the first leg. Emery talked to him more than once, even going so far as to ask him to do the impossible and play. 'We need a cool head, someone to take charge, someone with experience.' Right up to the last moment, the coach was hoping to be able to count on 'papa' Motta. To no avail. Adrien Rabiot was his obvious replacement, but he didn't train in the week before the match. Véronique, his mother and also his adviser, called the club one day: 'Adrien can't even get out of bed, and he can't eat anything.' He lost three kilos in a week, and dragged himself back to training on the Sunday, able to do no more than trot. The same story with Angel Di Maria, injured since the first match, and a doubtful starter. As if that weren't enough, Javier Pastore pulled out of the Sunday training because of his calf injury…

On the morning of the match, Pastore reported back to the staff. He said the injury was improving, but that he needed to put himself to the test. Di Maria and Rabiot were declared more or less fit, as there was no other choice. After the warm-up and lunch, the players went back to the hotel as normal. 'A few hours before kick-off, there was no great concern. The lads were super-confident', says Grunstein. 'We left a bit before them to get to the stadium and make sure everything was ready. When I left the hotel, I wasn't worried. The lads were on a winning streak, they were pretty calm.' This confidence was evident in all the corridors of the Fairmont Rey Juan Carlos I, where two of the top officials were wondering what bottle to open that evening… Then came the moment to leave the hotel. 'That was when everything changed. I think that was where the game was played and lost,' in the view of Romain. An eyewitness at the time, he's almost the only person willing to talk openly about what happened, PSG wanting to stay silent about that day, apart from questioning the refereeing. 'As we left the hotel, the players met a huge crowd. It was incredibly intimidating.' The time taken to get from the hotel to the Camp Nou seemed endless. A mob of Barcelona fans surrounded the coach, which had to force its way through with the aid of the police, amid boos, shouts, whistles, insults, and some thrown objects. The players looked on without saying a word, their caps pulled down over their eyes. Nobody spoke. 'They saw they weren't playing against Barça. They saw they were playing against Barcelona, against a whole city. They'd never imagined that.'

As they got off the team coach, the storm of booing started up again. One by one, the squad entered the ground, trying not to pay any attention to what was going on around them. Impossible. The images and the noise jangled in all their minds, as if someone was playing the tune by Justice, 'Stress', on a loop. 'Our only chance was to make this a hell for them,' admitted one of the Barcelona officials.

The warm-up on the field was a complete disaster. Some of the players complained that the balls were too new, most notably Kevin Trapp. They went back into the dressing room. Last words from Unai Emery. They fell on deaf ears. 'As they went out into the tunnel and then onto the pitch, I've never heard such a noise. It was dense, threatening. We didn't have eleven players against us, but almost 100,000 people.' The players' faces were pale. The entire team dropped back, missed their early passes. Emery stood up, already nervous. He waved at his defence to get higher up the pitch. No reaction. Luis Suárez couldn't believe his luck and opened the scoring in the third minute. The Camp Nou literally exploded; PSG had arrived at the gates of Hell.

Half-time: Barcelona were winning 2-0. Unai Emery and Juan Carlos Carcedo got together after 45 minutes of shouting themselves hoarse. Even the other assistant, the more restrained but equally excitable Pablo Villa, was beside himself, shouting at the defence and midfield to get higher up the pitch, as they had planned on the training pitch. 'Everybody was staring at the floor in the dressing room, there wasn't a sound,' recalls Romain. 'Unai gave his talk. He was calm, but he tried to wake them up. My feeling is that it made no difference. He could have insulted some of them, but I don't know if there would have been any reaction. After that, he asked Motta to speak.' Just as at Chelsea in 2015, when PSG went to win qualification even though Ibrahimovic had been sent off, it was Motta who took the lead. 'I don't remember exactly what he said, but one phrase has stayed with me. It was just before they went out onto the pitch again. He said to them, more or less: "You'll have to choose how you want to die: either we lower our heads or keep them held high." I don't know if he had had a premonition, and I'm not sure whether those were his exact words, but we did croak. That I do know.'

It got worse shortly after half-time when Neymar fell over Thomas Meunier in the box and Lionel Messi converted the penalty, and yet Edinson Cavani renewed their hopes by reducing the gap on the hour mark (3-1). It was a moment's madness, when Verratti threw himself into Emery's arms, screaming his lungs out. Sitting just by the bench, Thiago Silva's personal physio reacted almost hysterically, jumping out of his seat and insulting the ball boy in front of him, giving him the finger. Everyone linked to PSG seemed overwhelmed by their emotions. 'From the stands, they looked like little kids. You could see it in their body language. The only exception was Cavani. He just stood there, unmoving,' says Antonio Moschella, a journalist from Naples who was there that evening.

The Uruguayan star had already hit the post before he scored and was hoping to double his total in a counter-attack led by Di Maria. The Argentine striker couldn't accelerate as usual but had to weave his way through towards goal. That gave Mascherano, who was nowhere near as quick as him, the time to get back and put in a tackle. *El Fideo* had just seen Cavani calling for the ball on his right but didn't pass it to him. Just as he was about to shoot, the Barcelona defender threw himself at him, tripping Di Maria and making him miss completely. 'We couldn't see Edi from where we were, but we all saw Mascherano dive in. We all thought it was a penalty – and then two minutes later, Neymar scored from a free kick. The rest...' Romain Grunstein has no need to continue: everybody knows what happened next.

In the midst of the shipwreck, some stood tall. 'Either we lower our heads, or keep them held high,' Motta had said. It seemed that Kimpembe, Areola, Ben Arfa, Pastore and Cavani had heard him. Kimpembe above all, who showed impressive maturity at the final whistle and in the days that followed.

The training sessions in the Camp des Loges were silent, heavy affairs. The little groups that usually liked to spend time together after the sessions went home on their own. 'If we come out of this alive, we can create something new from this wound,' said Unai. 'There's no middle ground. Either we recover, or we go under.'

While Patrick Kluivert and Olivier Létang, the two men in charge of sporting relations at the club, went to ground, Nasser Al-Khealïfi asserted himself. He called in Unai Emery. 'When a group loses its confidence, the motivator has to be there for them. But what happens if the motivator himself loses some of his energy? How does he get it back?', asks Igor Emery, Unai's faithful brother. 'The only thing Unai needed at that moment was to feel that the president supported him.' They went through not only the Barcelona match together, but the whole season, and came up with a list of things to be improved, from the banning of the players' friends and family from the dressing rooms, to a review of the staff and the club structure. Exit Kluivert and Létang, *bom dia* to Antero Henrique, the former strong man at Porto.

Four years after Leonardo's departure, PSG had finally got an experienced sporting director. Henrique immediately asked the relevant questions and acted swiftly. Did the team get nervous when there were big matches? Dani Alves was brought in. Did the club need a new sporting and media icon? Hello Neymar. Did Unai want at all costs to work with Mbappé, the revelation of the previous season at Monaco? No problem: Luis Ferrer, the Argentine scout who had been working for PSG since 2009 and was becoming increasingly influential, took care of everything. He was the privileged intermediary with the Mbappé family, who welcomed Emery to his home in Bondy, in order to convince the player to choose PSG over Real Madrid or Barça, who on 30 August had put in a definite offer of 180 million euros to the Monaco board!

For several hours, Unai and the great hope of the French game talked football and only football. 'I want to win everything,' Mbappé told him. 'I want to become the best player in the world.' Already enthused at the idea of playing in the city where he was born, and at having as teammates Neymar, Cavani or Verratti, Mbappé was won over by the persuasive Unai, who was exactly as Luis Ferrer had described him: a manager who was demanding, passionate, painstaking, and above all, ambitious.

***

Naturally, a squad like PSG's creates an awful lot of gossip. Every action is studied, judged, picked apart, (over)interpreted. The same applied to the press conferences, of which Emery limited himself to the strict minimum. This frustrated most of his French observers and led to the accusation that the Basque trainer allowed himself to be dictated to by his players, in particular the Brazilians. All this when it had been mutually agreed between the club officials and the players that everything would be dealt with internally, strictly internally.

Although it's true that life with Neymar was complicated to begin with, the two men learned to appreciate one another, and to talk. It was never going to be a great love affair, but their relationship improved. Once even, the Brazilian came out late for the second half of a Champions League match at the Parc des Princes because he was busy talking to the coach, whom he hugged and gave a kiss on the forehead. 'You need time to get everybody to play together. The problem is that this is a profession where the notion of time is absent', Juan Carlos Carcedo correctly notes. 'Neymar and Mbappé are two phenomenal athletes. Their speed, their individual talent, has to be made part of a collective process, one that was different from what we were used to.'

From that moment on, PSG was transformed occasionally into an incredible counter-attacking team, something it had rarely attempted previously. 'The most important thing is balance. I want my team to be balanced, for them to control the game, its rhythm, the spaces on the pitch', says Emery. 'We try lots of permutations while still giving our players the freedom to create. But that means they have to cover, and that everyone understands.' Given Motta's injury problems, Unai changed the midfield by adapting to the strengths of Rabiot, the new sweeper who was also a skilful ball-carrier. This allowed him to continue into the other team's half, because Draxler and, above all, Verratti filled in and took up his position. Even with the changes, the trio combined, and took each other's place and vice-versa. A kind of rotating midfield, which Dani Alves joined with great pleasure, becoming one of the favourite playmakers.

With so much talent and so many possibilities, PSG were a delight to watch, particularly when the team's stars weren't being too selfish. By the end of the first half of the season, they had only lost two games, to Bayern (1-3) and to Strasbourg (1-2). As well as having the best attacking record in the group stages of the Champions League, the team completely dominated *Ligue 1*, which they seemed bound to win. Everything seemed to be going in the right direction, even if the late changes Emery made were not always understood, either by outside observers or even his squad. 'We planned to have rotations throughout the season,' says Carcedo in justification. He gives as an example the three players used in central defence, Thiago Silva, Marquinhos and Kimpembe, who each played two matches out of three in turn. 'Managing players like them was different, of course, but no more so than at Lorca or Almería. What I mean is that they're all men. They are simply more talented, and therefore offer us more possibilities,' concludes Unai, who adds one last additional thought: 'If someone tells me that this is a difficult profession, I reply that I prefer to have this sort of problem. They're not even problems, they're solutions waiting to be found. That's different.'

17.2

INTERVIEW WITH ROMAIN GRUNSTEIN

Romain Grunstein joined PSG in 2013 as assistant kit and logistics manager. After being promoted to head of the department, he left the club in summer 2017 at the end of Unai's first season. Living every day with the players and staff, he was 'at their service', as he himself says.

First contact

'First and foremost, [Unai had] a strong handshake. He introduced himself and his staff to all of us. He told us from the start that we were important. I've spoken to many people doing my job in *Ligue 1*, and most managers don't really give a… [*He pauses*] Sometimes, we're called storemen, like the guys who carry boxes in a warehouse. I respect our profession, but trainers in France look down on you, as if you're only there to carry boxes… But our job isn't just that. I've always seen our job as being able to allow the players and staff to enjoy the best surroundings for them to be able to express themselves. Unai has always valued what we do.'

A staff complementing each other

'What surprised me was how all the staff could be so vehement during training and the games, but then incredibly gentle when everything was over. You should see them during training, they're shouting all the time, and on the bench during matches, especially Pablo Villanueva, one of the assistant trainers. He insults the ref even before the game starts [*laughs*]. But then off the pitch he's the opposite, he's a sweetheart. I was closer though to Julen (Masach), the physio. He's the strong, steady one in the group. One day, he came to ask me: "I've got lots of stuff... Would it be possible for you to help me transport it? I don't want to bother you, because I know you've got other things to do." He was embarrassed, but it's my job to organise things like that. In theory, in France, the physio doesn't ask politely, he just tells you to do it. Julen and I used to chat a lot, he used to tell me stories about his Basque country, his life and so on. It was the same with Victor (Mañas), the video analyst, even though he's very discreet.

'Then there's Carcedo... I see him and Unai like night and day, good cop, bad cop. They complement one another perfectly, it's really a double-headed management team. In his talks, Unai gets passionate, talks loudly. Carce is calmer, he has a more moderate tone. Yet it's funny but I'm convinced that's a false impression, because if a player were to poke fun at Carce, I could see him taking off his jacket and saying, "Come outside and say that [*laughs*]." [...] I see the PSG staff like the five fingers of a hand, each one with their own personality. That allows them to manage all different sorts of player. Someone who's more reserved, like Cavani, confided a lot in Julen Masach, for example, because they're alike. Carcedo was probably closer to the young French players.'

Improvements to the training centre

'Unai didn't do anything revolutionary. One of the things he did straight away was to open up all the offices at the training centre, apart from his own, which was closed so that he could talk to the players privately. That meant that video analysts, the performance manager and the other employees could all talk to one another and see each other. He said he wanted us to have a dialogue, an exchange, and above all a team spirit. On the practice grounds he asked us to set up workout equipment, because that sort of exercise forms part of his method.

So, we put up a tent alongside the pitches [*laughs*]. He also gave Martin Buchheit, the performance manager, greater importance. He was the one who prepared all the food and energy drinks in the dressing room before, during and after the games. I should add that Martin was brought in when Laurent Blanc was in charge, because the guy doing it before used to leave Haribo sweets and strawberry Jell-Os for the players at half-time. Blanc took one look at him and said: "What's all this crap?"'

Individual meetings

'During one game at Lorient, there was the famous episode with Serge Aurier.[26] I was just behind them, and when Unai realised what was going in, he came up to Serge and whispered something in his ear. I don't know what he told him, but it wasn't funny. Serge looked down at the ground, he wasn't fooling around: he's someone who was always respectful, who was very much appreciated at the club. All the press wrote that Unai gave him hell in the dressing room after the match, but that's nonsense, he never did that. They sorted it out between them, in a private chat. That's typical of Unai, he doesn't criticise players in public. When he has something important to say, he asks everyone to leave: physios, assistants, officials, everyone. More than once he locked the dressing room door so that it was simply the players and him. He had already said to me: "we don't wash our dirty linen in public."'

The sandwich story

'During the warm-up for the game at Barcelona, Unai was in the dressing room. Both of us were there, but at some distance from one another, because the away dressing room at the Camp Nou is enormous – you could fit four teams in there [*laughs*]. I had my back to him and had finished all I had to do. There were still fifteen or twenty

---

26 On the bench, Aurier was told by Unai to replace the injured Thomas Meunier. The problem was that the right-back wasn't ready and didn't even have his shorts on. It took eight minutes to make the change.

minutes before kick-off, and as usual he was pacing up and down. I hadn't had much to eat that day, so I took out a sandwich smeared with mayonnaise and began to eat two or three mouthfuls. Unai came over to me: "Romain, you do a great job, it's important for the team, but I don't want the players to see you eating in the dressing room, because they're not allowed to." Given all the tension and pressure in the air, he could have bawled at me, but he didn't. I did something stupid, yet he began by reminding me of how important I was for the team, that I should remember what my job was. In the end, he said: "That's how we're going to win!" That gave me fresh motivation [*laughs*].

'That's what I learned from him: nothing is certain until it's finished. Before that game against Barcelona, we all thought we were the champions of Europe. But he spent the whole week bringing everyone down to earth: "We have to be confident, we have to play with confidence, but we mustn't lack respect for Barcelona. That's the biggest mistake we could make, and it would give them a jolt of pride. A wounded animal is always dangerous." He was right, and that was a lesson for me in my life now: as long as the peace treaty hasn't been signed, the battle goes on.'

18.1

LIVE BY THE SWORD

By mutual agreement, Unai Emery and Paris Saint-Germain decided to part ways after two years, a tenure that included one French championship, two French Cups, two League Cups and two Champions Trophies. 'We had a quiet dinner with the president Nasser Al-Khelaïfi and Antero Henrique. It was the best solution all round,' says Unai, who is not keen to say much about his memories of Paris. 'That's the past… I'm at Arsenal now, that's all that interests me. It's a bit of a bore to still hear questions about PSG, even if yes, I did learn there. I had to face new situations, new players, a new country, a new language, a different way of seeing football and so I came out of it with greater experience to use with Arsenal.'

Unanimously respected at the club for his integrity and hard work, Emery didn't succeed in getting PSG beyond the round of sixteen in the Champions League. The two games against Barcelona, especially 'that damn match' in the Camp Nou were bound to be the lasting images of his stay as manager.

'In the first leg, we played an almost perfect game, with eleven players focused and operating like a real team,' recalls Edinson Cavani. 'We were all united on the pitch. Then came the return match…' The Uruguayan doesn't finish his sentence, but everybody understands what he meant. 'The first leg was probably the greatest team display by PSG in all its history in Europe,' says Luis Fernández, who knows what he's talking about: he's the first French manager to have won a European Cup, with Paris in 1996. 'Then in the second leg it was the complete opposite. For many of those who love PSG the way I do, it was as if the sky had fallen in.'

Responsible, together with the entire club, players and the top officials included, Emery managed to reinvigorate the players, something that was far from a certainty. 'He has a real strength to take people with him and get them to take responsibility', says one of Nasser's advisers. 'On the other hand, I think he takes too much stress on himself. He has an anxiety creating, nervous personality. He never stays still, and that can have an influence in certain complicated situations where more calm is needed. Well, I'm saying that, but he's won three Europa League cups, so that can't have bothered his players at Seville.'

Unai's excitement on the bench is well known. In Paris, he had to calm down and adapt, in his day-to-day routine as well. 'At first we did lots of tactical work,' recalls Thomas Meunier, the Belgian international right-back. 'We used to stop practice for the slightest detail. There was lots of video as well, we used to stuff ourselves with it *(laughs)*. He gradually adapted to the team, because some players weren't used to it. The sessions became shorter, to get to the essential more.'

There are two ways of interpreting this. The first, that the manager didn't manage to get his squad to fully accept his way of working. The second, that the manager was intelligent enough to adapt to his players' psychological make-up, even if it meant making some concessions. 'We were accustomed to doing a lot of work on set pieces, like throw-ins and corners, but in Paris we cut back on that aspect,' Carcedo admits.

In some training sessions, the players laughed at the importance given to throw-ins, as if this was a waste of time. Some people might complain that the manager didn't have enough authority to get his message across, but that would be too harsh: there's nothing to be done with a footballer who thinks a throw-in is a waste of time, especially if he's a full-back. 'Myself, I've always liked working with videos and tactics,' stresses Cavani. 'That's what I learned in Uruguay, and then in Italy. I was used to it somehow, so it didn't shock me.'

In the end, there are pros and cons, as with every club in the world. Except that PSG isn't like any other team: it's the only one run by a state – the state of Qatar. That means it works in a different way to all the other European clubs. There's an organizational structure, of course, but it's divided between Paris and Doha, the capital of Qatar. And above all, this structure is constantly changing: the personnel running security, communications, the kit managers, Nasser's advisers, the managers (Antoine Kombouaré, Carlo Ancelotti, Laurent Blanc, Unai Emery), the staff and sporting directors come and go, are replaced or promoted without ever really understanding why. 'Several people have suffered depression or become burnt-out,' say some of the employees, visibly terrified at recalling these matters. 'People spy on each other, try to find out who is talking to whom, because there's often false information going around. The club is divided at every level into different clans. It's very heavy, and some guys really lose it. One year, they had to repatriate an employee from Doha to Paris as an emergency when we were over there…' Romain Grunstein, the former kit manager, adds: 'Vincent, who was my boss at the time, was burnt-out as well, he collapsed. We love this club, we're fans, but there came a moment when it was too much. Some people get squeezed like lemons.'

Off the record, some of the players laugh at this 'world of crazies' where people call the president to complain about the manager, the sporting director or the performance coach, and get their way. 'It's very hard for a manager to assert himself at PSG', complains Luis Fernández. 'It's not so much having to deal with the stars' egos, it's the context, the way the club is run. God knows, I love this club, but it's not always easy. We should all be pulling in the same direction, that of Paris Saint-Germain.'

One winter's evening, Fernández invited Emery for dinner. They talked for hours about their shared passion, as well as about a mutual friend, Marcelo Bielsa, because Unai wanted his number to call him. Before he said goodbye and went home, Fernández whispered some advice: 'Promise me just one thing. If you live by the sword, die by the sword. But die with your ideas.' Unai replied, laughing: 'Don't worry'.

During his second season at PSG, the Basque manager had, for example, said he wouldn't always play Lucas Moura. A lot of people at the club, the player included, thought that Emery would give in, considering what great friends Lucas was with Neymar, but no. 'With him, it's the best who play, not the friend of a friend', says Grunstein. A great runner, strong in individual duels and skilful in the box, Lucas, now with Tottenham, did not fit in with the style of play PSG met in the French *Ligue 1*, which consisted of attacking teams who brought all their men back behind the ball, leaving little space. Emery preferred Di Maria, Draxler or Pastore, even if his relationship with the last of these suffered from a lack of understanding. 'If he wanted to buddy up to Neymar, obviously he would have kept Lucas', explains one of the club's officials. 'He didn't do that and was clear with him from the start.'

As always, Unai called the player in to his office for a private chat; an office that a player like Di Maria also knew very well, as he always received an explanation when he didn't play. 'He communicates a lot with everybody,' Grunstein explains. 'I remember Giovani Lo Celso's first day. He arrived all timid from Argentina with his family. I welcomed him in the dressing room. Then he saw his idol, Di Maria, who took him under his wing, like Cavani or Pastore. At first, he was lost, on the pitch and off it. The PSG staff protected him, and in the second season he was almost always in the starting eleven and was in the Argentina squad for the World Cup.'

Lo Celso's progress was one of Emery's achievements, as were those of Alphonse Areola and Presnel Kimpembe, both world champions with the French team in 2018. 'I'd been following Lo Celso for years,' explains Luis Ferrer, the Argentine scout for PSG since 2009, who has become one of the key figures in the club's sporting structure. 'He developed as a playmaker at his club, Rosario Central. He could also play a bit further back, but he was especially good at making great final passes, at creating dangerous situations. He had incredible skill on the ball.'

Nobody can criticise Lo Celso's technical ability, even if he tends to take too many touches of the ball. Emery brought him into the team gradually, giving him time with the physio, Julen Masach, to follow a special programme designed to help him stand up to the big brutes of *Ligue 1*. In the practice games at the Camp des Loges, Unai put him in different midfield positions: left-hand-side ball-carrier, the same on the right, or playmaker during the drills of 4-2-3-1 during training. After that, he used him as cover in front of the defence when Thiago Motta was injured and Adrien Rabiot seemed unlikely to make progress in that position. 'Gio has real talent, he can do everything with a ball,' says Cavani. 'He always tries hard, plays for the team. He's an excellent teammate.' Not refusing any role, the playmaker fits in as a defensive midfielder, where he doubtless makes tactical mistakes but which he compensates for with his willingness and his ability to direct the game, like a *numero cinco* in the Argentine tradition. 'He had some very good games in that position,' recalls Luis Fernández. 'He's a good model for the young players, like Christopher Nkunku. They've always taken training seriously, been willing to listen. They seized their chance when others were injured or suspended, even in positions different to the ones they were used to.'

In the 4-0 win against Barcelona, Unai brought on Nkunku in the 70th minute to replace the exhausted Verratti, much to the astonishment of those on the bench, which included far more experienced players such as Javier Pastore. No matter, Nkunku might have been born only in 1997 and to have played only a handful of games at the top level, but he was the one sent on to face Barça's midfield, with a simple piece of advice: 'Play your game. I believe in you, play your game!'

The next year in the Champions League, PSG finally came top of their group and thought they might have an easier next stage. No such luck: for the round of sixteen they were drawn against the champion for the previous two years, Real Madrid. 'Unai has really bad luck,' comments one club official. 'Barcelona last year, Real Madrid this time, when we had finished first in the group stage…'

The away game in the Bernabeu was prepared for with special care. In the days leading up to it, the PSG staff gave no indication of the starting eleven. Unai though already had a plan, even if he said nothing – his way of keeping the pressure up on his squad in order to get the best out of everyone in training. In the hotel on the morning of the match, Emery went to talk to Thiago Silva, in private. He told his captain he would be a substitute that evening and explained why: he wanted a higher line of defence, with a left-footed defender to restart counter-attacks, and more action higher up the pitch. Taken aback, the Brazilian didn't say a word during the team meal, although that afternoon the news was already all over *L'Equipe*'s website. 'Everything seems to be common knowledge at this club, everything is leaked,' mutters Luis Fernández.

Unai went to talk to Silva's replacement, the young Frenchman Kimpembe, who had already played a heroic role the year before against Barça in his first Champions League match. 'Play your game,' Unai told him. 'If anything goes wrong, it'll be my fault, never yours. I want you to be yourself, I know you'll be good.'

In the midfield, where the 4-3-3 was unshakeable in defence and could turn to attack as the players saw fit, Emery surprised his squad by putting Giovanni Lo Celso in front of the defence. The experienced Thiago Motta, injured for a good part of the season (knee and ankle), was judged by the staff to be too much of a risk. This exasperated the vice-captain, who thought he was ready, despite only having played a few minutes in the previous four months. So it was Kimpembe and Lo Celso instead of the two Thiagos, as well as Yuri Berchiche on the left in place of the presumed first choice, Layvin Kurzawa, who was sent to the stands.

'Die by the sword…' Luis Fernández had told Unai a few weeks earlier; he never said a truer word. PSG played with character, taking risks on the counter-attack and denying Real Madrid the ball. Adrien Rabiot opened the scoring, then Ronaldo equalised just before half-time with a penalty marred by an offside. The person to blame, Lo Celso, who also lost the ball two or three times because he took too many touches. At half-time, the young Argentine looked glum, but was rebooted by the team and the PSG staff. More focused, more intense, he was the playmaker for a good part of the second half, when PSG had the ball. It was a different story when they lost it, but Verratti was there to fill the gaps.

As the minutes went by, PSG dominated and created chances that unfortunately were wasted out of selfishness (Neymar, Mbappé) or by a mistake; oh, that long pass from Neymar to Dani Alves charging for goal all on his own… Emery made one of his typical substitutions, introducing a second wing-back in the right-hand corridor. Bizarrely, he chose to take off Cavani rather than Mbappé, because 'he wanted to stretch the Madrid defence by allowing the French player to get around the back,' says Igor. Alves moved to the right-wing, but also worked in the midfield to increase the number of passes. 'It was a change that allowed our team to keep the ball more,' Fernández explains. 'We were on top at that moment and had several chances. But when you don't mark the great Real Madrid…' You are made to pay. Zidane also made a change, bringing on Marco Asensio on the left flank. He twice bamboozled Meunier, and the Spanish side ended up winning 3-1, although no one in the stadium would have been able to predict that outcome 10 minutes from the end. 'Emery took a chance, call it a poker wager, and he was right to do so,' says the PSG official. 'Even though he lost, his team wasn't humiliated. We were the equals of the future winners of the competition. That's to some extent the symbol of Unai's adventure here: if he had won that match or at least not lost it, he would have emerged incredibly strengthened because of the choices he made. When he lost, no matter in what fashion, it's the defeat people remember, and his choices were seen as mistakes.'

In the return game, without the injured Neymar and with Mbappé ineffectual, PSG lost without glory (1-2). The two Thiagos, in the starting line-up this time, couldn't do anything about Real Madrid's undeniable superiority. The dream was over yet again for Paris, and the season finished almost immediately afterwards, with the title already won.

For Unai Emery, fêted by the Parc des Princes and recognised as a 'chic type' [a great guy], this was the first time he had won a championship. Another addition to his honours, but also with a sense of failure, of impotence, already seen with Carlo Ancelotti and Laurent Blanc. Obviously, the manager must bear part of the blame, but he's not the only one, especially since he left a solid base for his successor, Thomas Tuchel, to work with. 'I give myself seven out of ten', says Unai, who offered a neat conclusion to a long interview with Marti Perarneu about his Parisian adventure. 'What's lacking? For my creations to be more complete creations. And for them to be more *my* creations.' He has no need to worry: that's all Arsenal are asking.

18.2

INTERVIEW WITH UNAI EMERY

U nai Emery didn't read *El Maestro* before it was published. He never tried to find out exactly what was in it, as that was one of the conditions of my project: complete freedom of tone, with absolutely no modifications. After all, the book isn't an autobiography or a collaborative effort, simply an authorised biography. Unai accepted the idea, with one stipulation: 'It would be good to have some criticism.

I'd like to read some, I think that's interesting.'

It's quite rare to hear a manager calling for negative views, especially so openly, but Emery has nothing to hide. As a conclusion to the book, it seemed logical to allow the main protagonist to offer his own views on his career and the reminiscences of the 40 or so colleagues consulted for the book.

What is football for Unai Emery?

'My life? [*laughter*] Obviously, it's my passion. When I'm asked to define football, I always talk about emotions, the heart, love. It's something you feel deep down inside when you enter a stadium, raise your eyes and look at the stands, the fans coming in. I like to make a tour round the pitch before games, to look at the architecture, the colours in the stadium, the sky, to feel the atmosphere growing. I like to know that every spectator has enjoyed their moments in the stadium, that they have been excited, have felt something together with their team.

'I'm a great believer in the exchange that goes on between the public and a team. Wherever I've been, I've tried to soak up the essence of the club, the town, and to transmit that to the players. I don't think you can play football and feel nothing.'

How did your arrival at Arsenal go?

'Well, I can't say too much about that, because it's too soon yet, but I'm very pleased. Very pleased to discover a new club, a new championship, a new country. I was immediately shown the history of Arsenal, which is very interesting. Apart from that, it's like the other positions I've had. Lots of individual talks with the players, the club's bosses, the staff who were here last year, so that I could listen, understand what works, what could be improved. When a coach starts at a new club, there's always lots of discussions, trying to understand things, settling down to work. So now I'm getting stuck in with my staff.'

Your former teammates say you were a player who found it hard to cope with pressure. In your book *Mentalidad Ganadora* you jokingly say you were a *cagón*, 'shit-scared'. Did you realise this when you were a player or only afterwards?

'When you're a professional football player, you have a responsibility. When that responsibility turns into pressure, it becomes negative. But if the responsibility is, in fact, a demand on yourself, then it's positive. When I was a player, all the pressures I felt, wanting to play well, the duty to perform, created a lot of anxiety in me. I didn't know how to manage that on my own. I think I was missing someone – a manager no doubt – who could teach me to control my emotions. When I said I was a cagón, someone who was scared, I was, of course, exaggerating a little. But I really didn't know how to manage that aspect when I was a player, and so when I became a trainer, I worked on it with my players because nobody had done so with me. I owed it to myself.'

How have you worked over the years to learn how to control yourself and to bear the inherent pressure of being a manager?

'My doubts and fears helped me to learn how to manage the pressures of being a manager and my work with the players. I've also relied a great deal on books about self-confidence and personal development. A lot of what I've read has allowed me to apply these ideas to the players, but to give you a full answer, I was already interested in studies about being a manager while I was still playing. Not many players study about training when they haven't yet retired from the game. I got my diplomas, and when I became a coach I read a lot more about psychology, group management, pedagogy, leadership, in order to overcome all the weaknesses I had as a player and to be able to put the ideas into practice with my future players…'

Are there any authors who particularly helped you in this learning process?

'Daniel Goleman (author of *Emotional Intelligence*), Manuel Vásquez Montalbán (a prolific Catalan writer), John Maxwell (a specialist in books on leadership). There's also one book I like enormously, *In Pursuit of Excellence* by Terry Orlick. There are lots of other authors I appreciate, I read a bit of everything, including books about football. At the moment I'm reading about Guardiola and I've also got the one on Simeone, but I haven't started that yet. I also have Bielsa's biography and I really liked the first books that came out about Mourinho, and football tactics in Portugal.'

The greatest trainers, in no matter what discipline, recommend books to their players, especially people like Phil Jackson or Gregg Popovich in the NBA…

'I've always offered my players books to read, although not to all of them. If I've found some books useful, I go and buy them and then target players they could be helpful to. In my first season at Valencia I bought two books for each player. However, there were thirty people in the squad, and I knew that some of them couldn't give a damn, they weren't really committed to the team. So, I told the players: "I've bought two books for each of you. Any of you who want them can come and get them in my office." Immediately afterwards, several players turned up: "Boss, I'd like the books you thought of for me." Not all the squad came, but a lot of them did. That was a moment that made me really happy. To see them in my office, asking for books, talking about what they had read… In all my teams, players have asked me to recommend books, especially Mata, but he's a special case [*laughs*]. When I was at Seville, I recommended Victor Valdes' biography to Sergio Rico, because it's a story about suffering, about the sacrifice needed to become a great goalkeeper. Sergio had his doubts at the start of his career, so I talked to him a lot, advising him not to speak to the press and to come with me at the end of the day to do extra training. At the end of the season, when we won the Europa League, his father wanted to come and see me to thank me. That was perhaps my greatest satisfaction.'

It seems you consider compliments about you as a person more important than those about your abilities as a manager.

'Yes, that's the most important praise, in my view. To hear that I'm a good person [*he pauses*] … In addition, they can tell me I'm a good trainer, that they've learnt from me, and that's what matters to me more than winning any title. I want that exchange, that sense of sharing with the player, that idea of being better. That's why I mentioned Sergio Rico's father. I also once met the father of David Soria, who was Seville's other goalkeeper, and he thanked me for all I had done. Those kinds of things move me.'

To return to your playing career, there's someone who seems to me fundamental in your development first as a player, and then as a manager: Mikel Etxarri.

'Of course! I called him when I was starting out as a trainer to ask his advice. He was passionate about his work, and passionate to talk to, but above all very meticulous about tactics. He had a winning character. I remember talking to him when Lorca won promotion to the *Segunda*. I thought our first objective was to make sure we stayed up, but he told me: "Unai, you should be thinking about promotion, not staying up." He had always had that mindset, or rather that positive mentality that is always seeking for the best. That's what I learned from him.'

Can you explain a little about the positive mentality you tried to instil in your players at Lorca following the 1-2 home defeat home in the play-offs to win promotion to the *Segunda*?

'I was sad after our defeat, but the next morning I got up and we all went down to the beach to do our training. We talked about everything that had happened. Then I said to the players: "We had an opportunity. It might be more difficult now, but it still exists, and we have to carry on thinking it's still there. We have to look for it, work on it. All this week, we're going to think we can win, we can play. We're going to be positive and to go for it as hard as we can." And in the end, that's what we did."'

That takes us back to the title of your book, *Mentalidad Ganadora*. For their first book, most managers choose an autobiography, but you preferred to write (with Juan Carlos Cubeiro) about psychology and group management. Why was that?

'When the book came out, I was in my fourth season at Valencia. We were third in *La Liga*, which was our objective, but down there, people want more. So, when the book was published, some in Valencia said: "How can he talk about a winning mentality when he hasn't won anything?" I told them: "Hombre, I have won! I went up to the *Segunda* with Lorca, and then to the *Liga* with Almería. I may not have won any titles with Valencia, but we managed to come third for three consecutive years, and to qualify for the Champions League, which was our objective. A winning mentality doesn't mean you have to win the whole time. It means you work hard all the time to win, you think only about winning. Then you may or may not succeed, but it's a mentality, not a consequence. It's a path, the way of thinking of winning, of working to win." That's what I tried to tell them in Valencia when the book came out, but they didn't understand me, or rather didn't want to understand that it wasn't simply about winning. After that I won the Europa League three times, so people could say I have a victor's mentality today, but it's not that! It's not the mentality of a victor, it's the idea you carefully cultivate in your mind, the path you take.

'To give you an example: when I was a player at Toledo, in the Spanish second division, two friends and I always filled out betting slips for the results. One weekend, we were playing at Elche. One of my friends and I bet on Elche to win, because that was logical – they were the favourites. I went to pay the girl who had to stamp my slip. She was a Toledo supporter, and she stared at me: "How can you put Elche down to win? How can you do that?" I really learned a lesson from her. How could I be playing a match thinking we were going to lose? That was the start of a learning process to change my mindset. [...] When we were in the *Segunda* with Lorca, I knew my players liked to bet as well. So, I said to the captain: "Show me the predictions you've made!" They had all filled in results for every match, and I saw that two of them had put down that we would draw: "No! You should always put Lorca down to win! You can't put a draw or a defeat! Whenever you're predicting our result, you have to put that we're going to win!" That's what I learned from my own experience as a player.'

To return to your career, do you remember 17 September 2006?

'Was that the game against Cádiz?'

Yes, when it was said that it could be your last game in charge of Almería if you lost.

'It's hard not to remember it, because we gave away a completely surreal penalty! [*laughs*]. In the end we won 2-1. I had decided to use two midfielders who were strong on defence. That's the doble pivote I used a lot at Seville, though not at Valencia. There I had one defensive midfielder and one attacking midfielder. But to get back to that game against Cádiz, that was really the start of our season: after that we had a series of good results, and in the end won promotion.

José Ortiz, the captain, has spoken of your chat before the first game in *La Liga* at La Coruña, when you told them you were going to throw dice to choose the starting eleven. I suppose that was a metaphor to show you had confidence in all the players, not just the best.

I remember it well. Before the game, I wanted to show I had confidence in the players who had won promotion with me. We had some new, talented players, but I also had the old ones who deserved to play in the *Liga*, so I told everyone: "I don't give a damn who starts! I know the team is going to play well; I know that because I have confidence in you!" I played most of those who had come up from *Segunda* [Bruno Saltor, Santiago Acasiete, Mané, Albert Crusat, Corona and Soriano] and we won 3-0.

'Important players such as Felipe Melo were subs. I knew that he was better than all the others, I knew it! But I wanted to show respect for the players who had won us promotion, so I talked to him face to face: "You need to be humble. I know you're very good and you're going to play. But today you have to wait, because these guys deserve to play." I waited until we had two games close together, one on Sunday and the next on Wednesday, to bring him on from the start. That was our fourth game, and I put him on instead of Corona. He scored, and we won 1-0 at Murcia. After that he started in every game, but I reminded him several times that I had to respect the group as a whole, and so did he, however good he was.'

Alberto Benito, the sporting director, said with a laugh that Felipe Melo came to Almería because he's crazy.

[*Laughter*] 'We signed him for two million euros, I think. He was young, 21 or 22, and had faced problems at Santander and Mallorca. We didn't hide that from our president, but Alberto Benito knew Felipe very well. He'd seen him with Brazil in the South American under-20s tournament, and knew he was a lad with problems. Obviously, it wasn't easy to sign him, but we succeeded. In a pre-season match, we played against Málaga and he had violent clashes with two of their players. The president called me and Alberto in: "Why did you sign that player? He's completely crazy, so why did you sign him?" We told him straight out: "If he wasn't crazy, we couldn't have got him! We have to work with the craziness in him, because he's very good." And at the end of the season, he left for I don't know how many million euros (13 million, to Fiorentina).'

How did you work with him to control his 'craziness' on a daily basis?

'Felipe talked a lot about his father as someone who had always helped him, so we discussed him a lot. But my talk was based on the idea of humility: "You're a very good player, but you need to stay humble if you want to progress." He would listen to me, he respected me, and we spent a lot of time talking together, just the two of us. In training, he liked to show he was the best, so I took advantage of that: "It's no use proving you're the best in training. All the other players know that, and they don't like it when you behave like that. You need to be humble with them, not to show off. It's on match day that you need to prove you're the best, on match day!"'

Among other players, there's Ever Banega, of course.

'Ever [*he pauses*] ... He is special. I had him at Valencia when he was younger, more immature, so I had to keep a distance from him in our discussions. But he was already a very engaging, very receptive lad: if you give to him, he gives to you. Quite often I had to be a bit of a father to him, to tell him certain things to get him to change. He always responded well, even if we had our arguments at Valencia; that's what happened with Miguel as well. That makes me think of something I read in *Marca* the other day. It was one of the nicest compliments I've ever had, from Steven N'Zonzi. He was explaining what he'd learnt from me as a footballer, but also on a personal level. With him it was the same, we had our clashes. I even kicked him out of training once in my first months at Seville! He came to see me, telling me he wanted to leave. I gave him three days off to think about it, to recover. He wasn't feeling good, he had personal problems and couldn't get used to the city. The following Monday, I asked him what he wanted to do, and he told me: "I'll continue!"'

All this to explain that with the players it's a process: a relationship isn't built in a day.

'As for Ever, I wanted to bring him to Seville. I said to Monchi and Oscar (Arias, the technical director), "If he plays the way he does, and if we succeed in getting him to play the way he can, he'll get the fans at Sánchez-Pizjuán out of their seats! He has to be looked after, to be given affection and love, but we also need to be demanding with him." After he arrived, I always quizzed him about his wife and his weight. Monchi also talked a lot with him: "What did the boss say?" "The boss is always asking me about my family and my weight. Every day!" [*laughter*] If everything is okay in his family and he is his proper weight, you can work with Ever. It's easy.'

With regard to your management of a group, Alvaro Negredo remembers a chat where you showed images of the opposing team without saying anything, simply staring at each of your players. Then you took one of them aside when he asked you if there was a problem.

'Gary Medel! Betis v Seville, we were winning 3-0 and the match ended 3-3 after he was sent off. I told him: "The same thing happened in the team talk yesterday! You were on the defensive, and it was the same in the match. You don't know how to control your emotions..." pitbull – that was what I called him, pitbull. One of their players provoked him, and he reacted just as he had done with me. So, we worked on that aspect.'

A lot of players have emphasized that you made each team-talk different...

'I try to find something new for each game, to change a few things, but I don't always manage it. For example, in my fourth year at Valencia, I asked the *utillero* (kit man): "Españeta, what should our tactics be?" And he said: 'We have to play tiki-taka!' That made the whole squad laugh. The aim is to make the talk interesting. It was the same at Seville, where I would read out passages from the books I was reading; sometimes I also used to tell them more personal anecdotes.

At others, I even used to talk just about one or two players, as with Joaquin, for example. He scored two goals in the first match of the 2010-11 season against Málaga, which we won 3-1. We began the second half of the season with a game against Atlético Madrid, and he hadn't scored another goal. Just before the match in the dressing-room at the Vicente-Calderón stadium, I spoke to him in front of everyone: "Joaquin, you scored twice on the first day, but it's been twenty games and you haven't scored again. When are you going to score, Joaquin? We need that! But to score, you have to go looking for a goal, you have to get into the box and want to score!" And he scored another two goals (the match ended 2-1 to Seville).'

Are you aware that some players said they were bored by your team-talks, and found them too long-winded? Aren't you afraid your message will get lost if you speak for too long?

'My brother used to tell me that some players were weary of my talks at Valencia. I always told them the same thing, because it had happened to me before at Lorca: "I give my team-talk, and if not everyone listens, I couldn't give a damn because if there's just one player listening to me one hundred per cent that's reason enough to give the talk!" At the end of the season at Almería in *Segunda*, we were travelling to Jerez for the thirty-fifth game, with the possibility of promotion very close, and so I told the squad: "My talks are very repetitive, so today I'm not going to give you one. I'm not going to give you any motivation speech.' We were beaten 0-3. The captain, José Ortiz, asked me: 'Boss, why didn't you give us a talk?" – "I've already given you so many I thought it might tire you today." "To be honest, I missed that talk, boss." When a player tells you that [*a long pause*] ... Some players couldn't care less, they just relax during the team-talk but there are the others, the ones who listen, who want to hear it and like it. What I want is to see my players react, and for them to talk, because they too have feelings and ideas. I like to learn, to share, with my players and with people in general.

'A friend who worked with me at Seville made a very true remark. He said, "I sit in the stands to see the game with twenty people around me. Nineteen of them say everything and nothing, talk about unimportant things. But there's always one who can give you good advice about something you hadn't spotted." You can learn from everyone! So, I want my players to talk, to express themselves. But going back to Almería, my talks lasted from thirty to forty-five minutes or even an hour, because the squad participated as well. I remember that once a player fell asleep [*laughs*]. It was Kalu Uche, and I didn't notice because I was so caught up in my talk. So, at Valencia, seeing that Miguel always came in last and hid in a corner, I would say to him: "Hey Miguel, don't fall asleep back there, because I'm watching you!"'

With regard to your frequent use of videos, I imagine you feel the same: as long as some players want to watch them, the others have to get used to it.

'I often used to ask Marchena, the captain at Valencia: "What did you think of the video? Was it good?" "Boss, it was very good. Some of them thought it was a bit long, but they won't forget it because it was a good session. I personally really want the video, and lots of the others feel the same. because we learn a lot. So as for those who can't be bothered to watch…" I've always thought the same. I have to do my best, not for everybody, because some people couldn't care less, but for the majority. As for those who don't want to listen, well, that's up to them. Football may be a game, but it's a serious game. Obviously, you don't always have to be serious, you have to keep that word 'game' in mind, and so I adapt. I always have a positive attitude in my videos and talks, but if I see it's not the right moment, I don't carry on, I change to something else. I know very well that at the end of my time at Valencia and Seville, playing every Wednesday and Sunday, there were so many talks and videos it could become wearisome. But all my players can see I put everything into the different aspects of my job. They watch half an hour of analysis of images, but they know that took ten hours of hard work. I think they respect all the work, even if it can be a bit tiring.'

Another part of your daily approach is to work on set pieces. You've often said that in your early years as a manager you were inspired by a game against Albacete.

'By César Ferrando, who also trained Atlético Madrid. It was a game in *Segunda*, Leganés against Albacete, when I was still a player. They had an incredible number of routines for throw-ins, corners and free-kicks. Our manager spent the whole time shouting at us, and I thought: "Shit, our coach doesn't realise they have all these moves prepared in advance, and we don't know any of them!" As a player I learned you have to work on every throw-in, every foul, and to study your opponent to know what they're going to do. That's also the reason why I look at the other teams so much. So, if players say I use a lot of videos and talk all the time, that's the reason! Because I lost that game against Albacete! I lost it, *joder*! My coach was shouting at me and the whole team during that match, so I said to him: "You shouldn't be shouting, but working hard like they do, studying videos of them to see what plan we should have. What are you shouting at me for? I don't know what to do because you haven't told me!" It's true I was playing badly, but that was because the coach didn't give me any advice, because he didn't know a thing. We didn't co-ordinate our moves, we didn't prepare any strategies. In the end, what I learned as a player served me as a manager.'

Together with your assistant, Juan Carlos Carcedo, it seems you get inspiration from other sports like basketball to develop your strategies for set pieces.

'He often showed me moves from futsal and commented on them. We took a lot of inspiration from that sport, but also from basketball on-screen. Of course, basketball is played with the hands and therefore it's much easier when it comes to precise details than when you're using your feet in a much bigger space. But that doesn't stop us from trying to innovate and to look at what's being done elsewhere, not just in football.'

Nearly all the people I've interviewed are full of praise for you, but I know that's not something you particularly like.

'I enjoy criticism! In my career, things haven't always gone well with some people. I've had arguments that have never been resolved. I can think of a friend I had at Lorca, Xabi Sánchez. We played together and were good friends, aside from the fact that we are both Basque [*laughs*]. Then I became the manager. I had three central midfielders for two slots. At first, I rotated them, then I realised that two of them were better, and so I used them for important games. Xabi Sánchez, my friend, played less often and no longer spoke to me. He put a stop to our friendship, and that's something that has always hurt me, because I never knew if it was my fault or his. Anyway, that was no way to end our relationship… It was the same with Paco Jurado, the next year in *Segunda*. He had been a friend when we played together at Toledo and we signed him for Lorca to complete the squad. I told him straight out, "You're our fourth striker. But if you show me you're better, then you'll play!" That December, he was really angry with me because he wasn't playing, and I had lots of problems with him, so we decided he had to go. It hasn't always been easy, from Lorca to Paris!'

Talking of Paris, how did you deal with a media environment that is so critical towards you? Do you think that had an unconscious influence on the club, on your players, or on you?

'I had to put up with the same thing back at Lorca! I was just starting out, I was thirty-four, and there were two journalists who criticised me all the time. On the day after we won 1-0 against Cartagena, I read the report by one of these journalists to see what he said. He tore us to shreds! I couldn't understand that, because we had won a very important and very difficult game: it takes something to beat Cartagena away in *Segunda B*! We played well too. So, I called the journalist and he told me his article was good: "What do you mean, good? You criticise us, whether it's a particular player or me, just when we're fighting to win promotion, and you work for a local paper! You should be backing us, and so should everyone else."

"No, no, there's nothing wrong with my article, I'm not criticising. […]" "Okay, fine, you're not worth the trouble. I can't talk to you!" I hung up, because whatever happens, that kind of person will always do the same. Afterwards I said to the sporting director, Pedro Reverte: "We shouldn't look at the press. We have to concentrate on our job, on winning, and forget what they say, because they're always going to criticise us." When we won promotion to *Segunda*, that same journalist came up to me and said: "I'd like to talk to you for five minutes." "Yes, yes, we can talk," I said. He looked a bit nervous. "What's wrong?" I asked. "I want to start again from scratch," he said. "I don't have any problem with that or with you. I'm the same person, I couldn't give a damn."

'The moral of this story is that you shouldn't change the way you behave. If I talk to a journalist, he may think he can do what he likes with me, that I'll give him information. But all I want to do is my job, and the press is part of football, I know. But I'm not going to become friendly with a journalist just so he'll say something nice about me.'

[Unai's words were compiled from a series of interviews with the author, when he was at Seville in 2015, when he was with PSG in Paris and soon after his arrival at Arsenal.]

CAREER STATISTICS: UNAI EMERY

Born: 3 November 1971 in Hondarribia (Spain)
Position: Left-midfielder

Playing career

1990–1995: Real Sociedad (Segunda B) – 95 games, 7 goals
1995-96: Real Sociedad (La Liga) – 5 games, 1 goal
1996–2000: Toledo (Segunda) – 126 games, 2 goals
2000–2002: Racing Club de Ferrol (Segunda) – 63 games, 7 goals
2002-03: Leganés (Segunda) – 29 games
2003–2005: Lorca (Segunda B) – 38 games, 1 goal

Managerial career

January 2005–June 2006: Lorca (Segunda B, then Segunda)
July 2006–May 2008: UD Almería (Segunda, then La Liga)
May 2008–May 2012: Valencia (La Liga)
May–November 2012: Spartak Moscow (Russian Premier League)
January 2013–June 2016 Sevilla (La Liga)
June 2016–April 2018 Paris Saint Germain (Ligue 1)
May 2018– Arsenal (Premier League)

Honours

Lorca
Promotion to Segunda: 2004-05

Almerìa
Promotion to La Liga: 2006-07

Sevilla
UEFA Europa League Winner: 2013-14, 2014-15, 2015-16

Paris Saint-Germain

Ligue 1 Winner: 2017-18
Coupe de France Winner: 2016-17, 2017-18
Coupe de la Ligue Winner: 2016-17, 2017-18
Trophée des Champions Winner: 2016, 2017

Individual

Miguel Muñoz Trophy (Segunda División): 2005-06, 2006-07
La Liga Manager of the Month: March 2014, January 2015
European Coach of the Season 2013-14
UNFP Ligue 1 Manager of the Year 2017-18

ACKNOWLEDGEMENTS

I've never been very good at acknowledgements, doubtless because I was afraid there would be too many people to mention. If I forget anyone here, I hope they'll understand. But the idea for this book would have been impossible without the help of many people.

First and foremost, Igor Emery. I know he likes discretion, but I have rarely met anyone so honest, sensitive and intelligent. He never tried to interfere in my choices, simply giving some suggestions in order to give the most critical and impartial view of Unai.

As for the others, thanks to all those who agreed to respond to my questions for their time, their trust and their memories. *In extenso*: Ever Banega, Iñaki Bea, Alberto Benito, François Miguel Boudet, Philippe Burle, Cala, Juan Carlos Carcedo, Coke, Albert Crusat, Omar Da Fonseca, François David, Laurent De Palmas, Emmanuel Dorado, Julien Escudé, Mikel Etxarri, Nicolas Faure, Sofiane Feghouli, Carlos Fernandez, Francisco, Fabrice Henry, Mikel Jauregi, Timothée Kolodziejczak, Evgeniya Larioshkina, Manuel Llorente, Clément Loubière, Mickaël Marsiglia, Juan Mata, Xavier Moro, David Navarro, Alvaro Negredo, Roberto Olabe, José Ortiz, Andrés Palop, Dmitri Popov, Alexis Prokopiev, Adil Rami, Juan Carlos Ramos, Pedro Reverte, Pablo Rodriguez, Carlos Romero, Bruno Saltor, Luis César Sampedro, Juan Sánchez, Fernando Soriano, Javier Terenti, David Villa, Vitolo and Unai Emery. A word also for Ruben Baraja and Ricardo Costa, even if we didn't have time to do the interviews: it's only a postponed match.

Thanks also to the press teams at Cannes, Alcorcon, Lugo (German Romo), Getafe (Luz Monzon), Almería (Juanjo Moreno), Schalke 04 (Sanli Yilmaz) and l'UAV Football Vic-Fezensac (Sami Loukil). Thanks also to Alex Rowen (Manchester City), Juan Ramon Morales (Séville) and Max Fischer (Lucerne), even if we didn't manage to do the interviews we wanted to.

Other people have been important in helping me carry out interviews: Francisco Empis, Simon Festinesi, Henri Galipon, Pedro Herrera, Paul Le Guen, Victor Oñate, Badr Slassi and Jeronimo Tormo. Thanks as well to all those who took the time to offer their advice and criticism when necessary. In no particular order: Mélanie Marcuccilli, Pierre 'Vittek' Vuillemot, Vincent Tanguy, Nicolas Cougot, Philippe Goguet, Benjamin Henry, Loïs Guzukian, Amandine Tabonet, Caroline Taudière, Lamia El Hanbali, the forum UD Almería SAD, and my dear mother, always ready to protest with her cat Duchesse at the slightest misplaced comma.

An enormous thanks too to Michelle Ivonne, whom I exploited for weeks in transcribing all the many hours of interviews in Spanish, a job that she accompanied with some very personal notes: ('Stop breathing into the recorder, *joder*!').

Finally, a word for my editor Bertrand Pirel, for his trust and his patience. Thanks to him, I can do what I most love in the world: tell stories (and play basketball, but then that's another story).

Keep the faith.